BEING A PRIEST TODAY

Donald J. Goergen, O.P.
Editor

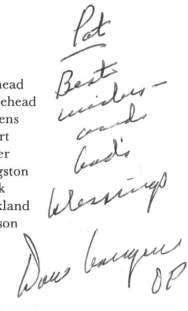

James D. Whitehead
Evelyn Eaton Whitehead
Donald B. Cozzens
Paul J. Philibert
David N. Power
Patricia H. Livingston
Matthew Clark
Rembert G. Weakland
Donna M. Hanson

A Michael Glazier Book
THE LITURGICAL PRESS
Collegeville, Minnesota

A Michael Glazier Book published by The Liturgical Press

Cover design by David Manahan, O.S.B.

1   2   3   4   5   6   7   8   9

Library of Congress Cataloging-in-Publication Data

Being a priest today / James D. Whitehead . . . [et al.] ; Donald F. Goergen, editor.
    p.   cm.
    "A Michael Glazier book."
    ISBN 0-8146-5032-5
    1. Catholic Church—Clergy.   2. Priesthood.   3. Catholic Church—Clergy—Religious life.   I. Whitehead, James D.   II. Goergen, Donald.
BX1912.B395   1992
262'.001'7—dc20
                             92-4819
                             CIP

To
Michael Glazier

Contents

Introduction

Donald J. Goergen, O.P.

A recent historical study that has been of service to the Church is Kenan Osborne's *Priesthood: A History of the Ordained Ministry in the Roman Catholic Church.*[1] One of the points he makes is the need to ground a theology of priesthood in Christology.[2] Ministry in the Church is the ministry of the risen Christ.[3] The Christological foundation of ministry was also emphasized at Vatican II in the council's focus on Jesus' threefold ministry as prophet, priest, and king. Jesus' threefold ministry was the basis for understanding episcopal, presbyteral, and diaconal ministry as well as the ministry of all the baptized (*Lumen gentium* 10–13, 20–21, 25–31, 34–36).

This threefold way of describing the ministry of Jesus or the ministry of the Church has varied.[4] Eusebius of Caesarea, in the fourth century, noted that *christos* means "one anointed" and indicated that priests, kings, and prophets were the anointed ones within Judaism, and thus that the Christ of God was also priest, king, and prophet. John Chrysostom applied these three roles to the baptized in commenting on 2 Corinthians 1:21–22. The patristic period did not use this threefold way of speaking to describe the ministry of bishops (*episkopoi*) or priests (*presbyteroi*). Thomas Aquinas (*Ad Rom.*, lect. 1; *ST*, 3, 31,2) spoke of the three titles as applicable to Christ but did not use them to elucidate his theology of the priesthood.

John Calvin, in his *Institutes of the Christian Religion*, was the first theologian to give an extended treatment to this tripartite way of interpreting the ministry of Jesus and in doing so gave it a more central role in theology. Calvin also applied this way of speaking to all the baptized. Not until the nineteenth century did Catholic theology apply this threefold pattern to the roles of bishops and the pope. Pius XII, in *Mystici corporis* (1943), used this threefold way of speaking to describe the role of bishops. Yves Congar, in his *Lay People in the Church* (1953), extended the three titles to all the baptized.[5]

Thus the threefold way of understanding "the anointed ones" of Israelite and Judean history has been variously used in Christian theology to systematize the ministry of Jesus, the ministry of all the faithful, ordained ministry, some of these, or, as at Vatican II, all of these.

I myself have never found this threefold way of speaking overly helpful, since the earthly Jesus was neither priest nor king and even seemed particularly ill at ease with the latter. Yet we are aware that ministry in the Church, ecclesial ministry, whether of the ordained or of all the baptized, must be grounded in the mission and ministry of Jesus Christ. Christology is the foundation of ecclesiology. So let us take a brief look at this foundation.

1. *The risen Christ.* One of the more effective starting points for Christology today is the risen Jesus, the resurrection of Jesus, Jesus as raised from the dead.[6] One of the consequences of the resurrection of Jesus and the appearance experiences of the disciples is that Jesus was recognized and proclaimed as "the Christ" (Acts 2:36). For Paul, in fact, Jesus only became the Christ as of his resurrection from the dead (Rom 1:4).[7] For Mark, it seems more likely that Jesus was understood to be the Messiah or Christ as of his baptism (Mark 1:9-11), and for Matthew and Luke, as of Jesus' conception in the womb (Matt 1-2; Luke 1-2). Anyway, the public proclamation of Jesus as being the Christ of God began after the resurrection of Jesus and the gift of the Spirit. Once Jesus

was recognized or understood to be the Christ, *the* Anointed One, it became theologically understandable that Jesus would be seen as the fulfillment of the anointings of the first covenant, the anointings of prophets, priests, and kings.

Once Jesus was proclaimed as the messiah, in what did the messiahship of the risen Jesus consist? There were three prominent interpretations of the messiah in intertestamental Judaism, based on interpretations of the Hebrew Scriptures: the royal, prophetic, and priestly messiahs. Some expected the messiah to be a king, another David, a king like the kings of old who would gather all the tribes of Israel together and rule over the nations—the political messiah. Others, including the Samaritans, expected not another king for Israel but a new prophet, another Moses, or another Elijah who would speak in the name of God (Deut 18:15-18; Mal 3:1; 4:5-6). In addition, there was also the expectation for the priestly messiah, or Levitical messiah, rooted in the vision of Ezekiel and his hopes for a renewed priesthood and restored Temple.

It is in this context, then, that the threefold ministry of Jesus takes on meaning. There are three faces or functions or ministries of the risen Jesus, the risen Christ. Jesus, both Lord and Christ (Acts 2:36), as raised from the dead, is our true prophet, new high priest, and only king. Thus the ministry of the *risen* Jesus, that is, the ministry of the Church, of all the baptized as well as ordained ministers, can be described as prophetic, priestly, and royal—as a ministry of the word, a ministry of sacrifice and sacrament, and a ministry of pastoral leadership. And yet, to understand the ministry of Jesus, and in turn the Church's ministry, we must push ourselves beyond our understanding of Jesus as the risen Christ and go further.

2. *The incarnate Word.* The Johannine Christians in particular came to the unique understanding of the Christ of God as the Word of God incarnate. This understanding of Jesus within the context of a theology of the Word gives another focus to the nature of ministry. All ministry is ministry of the

Word. It involves the enfleshment of God's very own self-communication. There is in all ministry a certain *communicatio Dei*.

All ordained ministry is an intensification, exemplification, sacramentalization of the ministry of the Word. According to the teaching of the Second Vatican Council, presbyteral ministry has as its primary responsibility the proclamation of the Word (*Presbyterorum ordinis* 4). The specific focus of presbyteral ministry is God's Word—the Word enfleshed in Jesus, written in the Scriptures, contained in the Catholic tradition, proclaimed by the Church, and present in our human experiences.

3. *The earthly Jesus.* If a theology of priesthood is grounded in the theology of Jesus Christ, if there is always a Christological foundation for the theology of priesthood, then especially today that theology must take into account the earthly Jesus, whose life and death, whose mission and ministry, evoke powerful responses. If the risen Jesus, the risen Christ, helps us to understand presbyteral ministry, so certainly does the earthly Jesus, the earthly Christ, for indeed the risen Christ *is* that selfsame Jesus of Nazareth and that Jesus of Nazareth *is* God's Word incarnate.

Whereas exalted expressions describe the resurrected Messiah, other descriptions more aptly and accurately depict Jesus the Nazarean. These, too, inform our theology of ministry. Jesus of Nazareth is better understood as a prophet, sage, and servant:[8] so likewise the presbyter. Jesus was a courageous and prophetic preacher who preached in word and deed, whose prophetic, symbolic actions equaled the power of his enigmatic sayings and provocative parables. Jesus was a compassionate teacher of wisdom, and the traditions of both prophecy and wisdom are necessary to help us understand him. In many ways Jesus was like the prophets and sages of old, and yet was perceived as greater than Jonah, greater than Solomon, and even greater than Moses and Elijah. In his tragic death, Jesus, God's servant, became the victim of historical, social, political, economic, and religious forces and died a martyr's death. This earthly Jesus—prophetic preacher, compassionate sage, servant of the gospel—gives us another way of talking about ministry in our own world and our own period of history.

Jesus was clearly "from God," "of God," and yet so utterly human. He was absolutely in solidarity with God, was God, and yet totally in solidarity with humanity, with people, especially the socially marginal, economically disadvantaged, and religiously alienated. Jesus was a man who taught what he lived and lived what he taught—a man of unsurpassable integrity and freedom. He loved his God with all his heart, all his soul, and all his strength, and he loved people as much as himself, even to the point of laying down his life. This is the content of the earthly ministry of Christ.

4. *The death of Jesus.* Jesus' death on a cross epitomizes the ministry of Jesus and the mission of the Word. The cross captures Jesus' radical solidarity with the victimized of the world and the degree to which his sacrificial love for others and for God would go. The presbyter too must stand in solidarity with victims of suffering and exemplify the kind of love to which God calls us, the kind of love that God is. Our *imitatio Christi* becomes a *communicatio Dei*, whose very being is revealed as being for others. Discipleship is servanthood, and ecclesial leadership is a particular way of being a disciple. The leader is first and foremost a disciple, a servant, one whose primary call is to follow after Jesus, the risen Christ. The presbyter shares in the mission and ministry of the risen Christ—as prophet, priest, and leader. As a disciple of Jesus, his ministry also models the mission and ministry of the earthly Jesus— a prophet, sage, and servant. The presbyter also makes present to our world and our period of history the mission and ministry of the Word. The presbyter preaches in word and deed while sharing in ministry with all those who are called through baptism to share in this ministry as well.

These Christological foundations should be elaborated at greater length, but my purpose here is only to remind us that the sources of a renewed theology of the priesthood lie in Christology and in pneumatology. The primary gift of the risen Jesus to his followers was the gift of the Spirit.

*   *   *   *   *

In this collection of essays, Donald Cozzens makes the point that the continuing wellbeing of the Church is intimately connected with the continuing wellbeing of its ordained ministers. We are increasingly aware, theologically and pastorally, that the Church is God's people, the community of the faithful. A people-centered Church does not deny the importance of ordained ministers, although serious adjustments must take place. The Church is in the process of discovering this new identity for its ordained ministers.

The challenge is not only an academic one, not only a pastoral one, but also a spiritual one. For all baptized Christians, appropriating and deepening life with Christ in modern secular culture is a formidable and urgent task—the quest for truth and life grounded in the gospel. It is that same quest that the ordained priest must undertake at a level of profound commitment. What does it mean to be a presbyter among all the disciples of Jesus Christ? The ordained minister is first and foremost a disciple of Jesus Christ. Nor are presbyters the only disciples called to leadership. What is the particular form of leadership to which the presbyter is called? These are the kinds of questions to which the essays in this book are addressed.

These essays cannot cover the full range of biblical, historical, theological, pastoral, psychological, sociological, and cultural issues involved in the contemporary development of the Roman Catholic priesthood. The contributors to this collection have addressed, however, a variety of concerns.

James Whitehead directs our attention to the present crisis as a call to the Church as an institution for an ongoing purification. At issue is the priest's sense of belonging, and thus identity, where the priest belongs in the community of faith. Evelyn Eaton Whitehead calls attention to ministry as both a vocation and a profession, and she explores the ministerial accountability of the priest as a public person.

Donald Cozzens addresses the issue of a presbyteral spirituality for diocesan priests. He writes, "The decision to pray is arguably the most important decision the priest makes concerning his spiritual life." The priest prays that he might preach, but also preaches that he might pray. His spirituality is worked out in this dialectic between preaching and prayer.

Priesthood, however, is expressed in varied ways. It is not some kind of genus in which there are two species of priesthood: diocesan and religious. The starting point for understanding religious who are also presbyters is religious life itself. This is their primary identity, not their priesthood. Paul Philibert sheds light on the growing awareness that religious life provides a contrasting context for interpreting priesthood. For Philibert, religious who are also priests confront symbolic dislocation on two fronts: religious life as a personal identity and priesthood for religious as a role or office in the Church. Religious are symbolic persons, and this is central to any understanding of religious who are ordained.

David Power explores the theology of priesthood and contemporary issues associated with it through his theological and historical analysis of the priest as one who acts *in persona Christi* and *in persona Ecclesiae*—helping us to see how these two expressions need not be in opposition to each other but are integral to each other. The mystery of Christ and the mystery of the Church cannot be separated.

The varied contributions in this collection offer varied images for understanding ordained priesthood and various issues that need continued reflection. Patricia Livingston speaks out of her experience of ministry to priests. She focuses on three issues every priest must face: integration, ministry, and spirituality. Bishop Matthew Clark writes about the priest as a pilgrim among pilgrims. His is a challenging essay that respects both the gift of ordained priesthood and the gift of celibacy but articulates the concern about mandating their being joined together.

Archbishop Rembert Weakland addresses the challenging issue of the priest's call to do justice. Donna Hanson talks about priesthood as accompaniment and the priest as a learning teacher, wounded healer, and enabling servant.

One of the greatest challenges presbyters face today is the struggle for integrity, confronted as they are by the gospel they proclaim. To be faithful, to live what one proclaims, to be the human face of God's divine presence to people, is never easy. It is as demanding as it is rewarding.

How do we ecclesial men and women help our Church to move beyond every vestige of triumphalism so that we as Church more effectively serve the gospel? In an age that is secular and religiously pluralistic, a sense of triumphalism and superiority gives false witness. We, however, are called to ministry for the sake of the gospel. How does the presbyter in particular give witness today?

How do we move our ecclesial analysis beyond the false context imposed by ideological extremes? The challenge that confronts us most strongly is not the liberal-conservative division of the Church but whether we can find a proper ground on which to seek the truth, whether we are able to do justice to the majority of our people by refusing to let extremes determine the context of our discourse, whether we are able to hear the gospel's word to our society or only hear the gospel within an ideological framework provided by our society. The future of the Church, of God's presence in our history, will be neither liberal nor conservative. Our most radical commitment must go beyond ideologies that divide us and that give allegiance to their own self-interests.

How can we get angry with ourselves, with our Church, and yet as preachers, teachers, and leaders move beyond that anger? There was probably no one in Church history more conscious of corruption in the Church and among the clergy than Catherine of Siena and yet no one who loved more the Church she also challenged. One of her metaphors spoke of the Church as full of leprosy, and her struggle, literally and ecclesially, was to embrace the leper. How do we reach out and embrace that which causes us pain and disappointment?—an urgent question for anyone who loves. Can we sacrifice together to build that which we will probably not live to see? Can hope rather than anger be the basis from which we build?

The media ordinarily trivialize the priesthood or publicize scandal. Rarely is attention given to the many who have freely and healthily chosen self-sacrifice for the sake of the gospel. Yet the media make the world in which we live. Our reality is the one they create. The reality that most people know about the Middle East or Central America or the poor or the Church is the reality given them by the media. How can we as Church through our communities of faith, our liturgy, and our proclamation provide another context in which people can live and interpret and understand the mystery of their lives?

These are the kinds of questions with which I personally struggle, the kinds of questions with which all baptized Christians must struggle, especially those called to ministry in the Church. Our love for the gospel we are called upon to serve and our love for the Church who is called to serve that same gospel provide our greatest satisfactions and our greatest challenges. It is only our solidarity with Jesus Christ that will enable us to hold out and win through. I hope that these essays will help presbyters in the Church to deepen their solidarity with the risen Jesus.

Notes

1. Kenan B. Osborne, *Priesthood: A History of the Ordained Ministry in the Roman Catholic Church* (New York: Paulist, 1988).

2. Ibid., 3-29, 317-318.

3. ''The risen Jesus continues his ministry in and through the Church's ministry, and therefore a study of Church ministry is in reality a study of the ministry of the risen Lord.'' Ibid., 29.

4. Cf. Peter J. Drilling, ''The Priest, Prophet, and King Trilogy: Elements of Its Meaning in *Lumen gentium* and for Today,'' *Église et Théologie* 19 (1988) 179-206. See also Osborne, *Priesthood*, 308-315.

5. Yves Congar, *Lay People in the Church: A Study for a Theology of Laity,* trans. Donald Attwater (London: Geoffrey Chapman, 1957).

6. Cf. Donald Goergen, *The Death and Resurrection of Jesus* (Wilmington, Del.: Michael Glazier, 1988); Gerald O'Collins, *Jesus Risen* (New York: Paulist, 1987); Franz Josef van Beeck, *Christ Proclaimed* (New York: Paulist, 1979).

7. Cf. James D. G. Dunn, *Christology in the Making* (Philadelphia: Westminster Press, 1980) 33-64.

8. Donald Goergen, *The Mission and Ministry of Jesus* (Wilmington, Del.: Michael Glazier, 1986).

Priestliness: A Crisis of Belonging

James D. Whitehead

Priesthood in the United States has come to a crisis. The details of the distress are now familiar: a nearly 40 percent drop in the number of diocesan priests in the past twenty-five years; the dramatic increase of priestless parishes; an evident loss of confidence among priests themselves. But in naming this painful experience a crisis, do we illumine our distress or simply trivialize it?

"Crisis" for many Americans functions as a cliché; at the national level, for example, our legislators acknowledge that the economy is in crisis and yet continue with business as usual. At the personal level, claiming a mid-life crisis seems to excuse erratic behavior. Crisis-as-cliché condones disruptive actions instead of clarifying the discipline of change that we must face. But acknowledging a crisis may also guide a healing exploration of the mysterious dynamics by which God is purifying our life of faith.

Crisis as Religious Purification

Priests and ministers are familiar with crisis. Specialists in other people's pain, they recognize how this dynamic of loss can be a part of growth. Priests learn again and again in their pastoral ministry that a crisis is not an abandonment by God but an avenue for God's intervention. As Church leaders, we have come to appreciate crisis as one of the ordinary ways that God finds access to the human heart. But when a crisis threatens us personally, our professional wisdom may desert us. Facing a painful loss, we forget the hard-won conviction that life comes from death. So recalling the dynamics of crisis may illumine the current pain of the priesthood.

The Threat

A crisis begins, whether abruptly or gradually, when an essential part of life fails us. For years we have been comfortable in our work, clear in our relationships with others, settled in our spirituality. Then, some part of this accustomed stability no longer "works." We begin to feel dislocated, disoriented. Negative feelings stir within us: embarrassment—what is wrong with me? Hurt—this is not fair; this should not be happening.

At the beginning of a crisis, the threat is strong but often obscure. What is going wrong? Why do I feel so bad? The danger is urgent but has no name. What is in peril? What part of my life is being stripped away? Only gradually do we become aware of the loss that threatens our life. As ministers, we have seen this process so often in the persons we care for. The illness of a child or the stagnation of a marriage brings panic to a person's heart. God cannot be doing this to me!

At the onset of a crisis, the virtues of patience and courage are most in demand. Patience to listen to what is happening; courage to face the loss that threatens our survival—these virtues are possible only if we can believe that God is present here. Faith sustains our confidence that a crisis is not the punishment of a vindictive God but the intrusion of a God who leads us down strange paths toward new life.

Privatizing the Pain

But even with faith, holding still in a crisis is difficult. We are tempted to avoid the pain, to turn away from this loss. Some people bury themselves in work. Others turn to alcohol or drugs to medicate the pain, or we slip into a depression—a nameless heaviness and sadness that barely masks the pain we refuse to face.

Evidence of this crisis behavior abounds in the Church these days. As a priest feels a depression descending on his life, for example, he often blames himself. "If I were more generous, if I prayed more, if I were stronger . . ." Privatizing his pain, the priest assumes the problem must be his. Institutions in crisis are sorely tempted to support this personalized interpretation. If the pain can be kept private, the remedies will be private as well—psychological counseling, a long retreat, sabbatical leave, an extended vacation. An organization feeling its structures and survival threatened may determine that private remedies are less costly than institutional reform.

Treatment facilities for disabled priests spring up around the country. But as the number of troubled priests mounts, a more awful truth insinuates itself into some hearts. What if this pain is more than private? What if these troubled lives are symptoms of an organizational structure that no longer works? If patience and courage are demanded to face a personal crisis, these virtues are even more in demand to confront an institutional threat.

A special bias in Christian life supports a reluctance to acknowledge the institutional crisis in the Catholic priesthood. Though we confess that ours is an *ecclesia semper reformanda*, this constant call to purification is often interpreted as pertaining solely to individual believers. In this interpretation, while the individual priest will always need to acknowledge failure and grow in holiness, the institution stands outside the reform process. The institutional Church, as divinely constituted, is exempt from an ongoing purification. Or is it? Do not the leadership structures of our faith community—our established procedures of selection, formation, and accountability—also stand under God's judgment? Do not these structures, developed under God's guidance but built by human hands, always await cleansing and healing? Is any part of Christian life exempted from the paschal mystery—that we come to life, repeatedly, by dying to what we have considered most precious?

The Decision

In psychologist Erik Erikson's phrase, crises "make patients of us all." Crises are disruptive events: We do not choose them and we do not want them. Yet they happen. We can resist crises, but we cannot completely avoid them. The New Testament word *krisis* means "decision." In a time of crisis we are called to decide: We must identify what is being lost, let go this accustomed part of ourselves, and open ourselves to new possibilities. But to define a crisis as a time of decision seems a cruel joke. In the midst of our distress, we are so bewildered and confused that choice seems impossible. Our usual criteria for deciding have deserted us; we do not know where to turn.

Yet when we examine the experience of crisis more closely, we recognize the choices involved. A first choice can be to skirt the crisis. We can refuse to enter this purification and instead lose ourselves in work or some other diversion. We can decide to "tough it out," denying both the pain and the purification. This choice leads individuals and institutions toward stagnation.

In another choice we may enter the dark passage of a crisis and fail to come out of it. Clinging to a part of ourself we cannot let go, we become stuck in the middle of this transition. The classic example of a crisis-become-chronic is the grieving parent who keeps the dead child's room as it was. The parent cannot, does not make the decision to let go. Instead, the person refuses to form a new relationship with this precious but changed part of his past. Here, crisis becomes not a passage but a way of life.

In the New Testament a crisis is also an end-time. In John's Gospel *krisis* refers most often to God's final judgment, that decisive moment that ends history. But every crisis ushers in an end-time: Some cherished part of ourself is dying; a portion of our identity that we cannot do without is being taken away. This end-time, this *eschaton*, brings good news: It is a time of God's special presence. Our God, whom we picture as dramatically present in the final judgment, is acutely present in the other crises of our lives. Shorn of the distractions and secure identity of our well-defended lives, we are laid bare to God's advance. Through this rupture in our accustomed lives, God finds a route to our hearts.

At the core of a crisis stands that most threatening question: Will we survive? In the priest's ministry, he has heard the question asked many times before. A father is convinced he cannot survive the death of his only child; a woman knows she is unable to live without her spouse. In crisis himself, the priest may fear that he cannot survive the loss of a sense of his "specialness," so essential to his priesthood. Yet, in these crises, God invites us to let go of what we are convinced we cannot do without. These essential parts of our life are cut away, not because they are bad or sinful. They are taken from us because they are not part of God's future. For a believer, any serious crisis will become also a crisis of faith. "How can God act this way? This is not the God I have always believed in." So, in the pain of a crisis, we lose a faith that once fit our life but now fails us. In its place a new and deeper faith begins to grow.

Naming the Loss in the Crisis of Priesthood

A crisis waits to be embraced. We become partners with God in this purifying drama when we look into the turmoil and attempt to name the peril we face. The threat to the institution of priesthood is about *belonging*—where and how the priest belongs in the community of faith. Belonging includes questions of social position, esteem, contribution, and sacrifice. For centuries the priest belonged as a member of the clergy and as a "sacred person" in the community. That is, his social position set him apart from the laity as a specially chosen man of God. This position of privilege came with a required sacrifice: celibacy. In the world of Catholic faith before Vatican II these dynamics supported many holy and effective priests in a challenging and rewarding vocation. As priests, they knew where and how to belong.

The transformations wrought in Vatican II jeopardized the place of the priest in the community. As Edmund Hussey has described in his excellent article "Needed: A Theology of Priesthood" (*Origins*, Feb. 4, 1988), the council urged both bishops and the laity to a more energetic way of belonging. Bishops came out of their authoritarian seclusion to become more pastoral and more directly involved in the diocese; the theology of the council pictured the bishop as the chief pastor and the priest as his assistant. The laity suddenly began to minister to one another, doing many of the things once reserved for the priest. Both these healthy developments encroached on the priest's position in the community; both have contributed to the crisis of belonging in the Catholic priesthood.

Transformations within the priesthood itself were influencing the way the priest belongs. Robert Schwartz discusses (*Origins*, June 14, 1990) the way the priest's role quickly changed from cultic specialist to orchestrator of the community's gifts. The priest's ministry had once been as simple as the sacraments: Mass, confession, weddings, and funerals defined his ministry and set his daily schedule. In the 1960s, ministry exploded in response to new pastoral needs; the community leader could no longer supply these needs but had to coordinate a community's response to them.

Theologians Edward Kilmartin, David Power, and others trace the less-obvious shift in the priest's symbolic position in the community: from the group's unique representative of God (as *alter Christus*) to the leading representative of the group's faith before God. The loss and gain of these shifts have been felt by most priests. As orchestrator and representative of the community's faith, the priest finds himself in a more intimate relationship with other believers. But he has also lost the privilege and the guaranteed legitimacy that his role once insured. He is compelled to belong to the community in new and unfamiliar ways.

How We Belong: Clergy and Laity

For centuries the priest's place in the Church was as a member of the clergy caring for Christian laity. Vatican II's recovery of the potency of baptism puts this ancient distinction at peril. To become religious adults, the baptized must *do* their faith. To mature into the full adulthood of Jesus Christ, lay Christians must do more than cling to their religious convictions. They must express their faith in actions of justice and love. This adult need makes ministers of us all. But as ministers, the laity "trespass" into the domain once reserved for the clergy: Lay Catholics today are teaching religion, visiting the sick, preparing others for the sacraments of initiation and marriage, even preaching. Priests are often left wondering where they belong.

Church historian Alexandre Faivre, in *The Emergence of the Laity in the Early Church*, reminds us that the familiar distinction between clergy and laity is not as ancient as the Gospel. For several generations in the early Church, community leaders as presbyters enjoyed no special status or life-style. Restrictions governed their selection ("The presiding person must have an impeccable character and must not have been married more than once" [1 Tim 3:2]), but as yet no distinctive class of clergy existed. *Laos* still bore its inclusive New Testament meaning: all the people of God.

Church leaders first crafted the novel distinction of clergy and laity in the third and fourth centuries. As presbyters took on the new title of "priest," they also assumed a new social status as clergy. In the following centuries the familiar features of clerical status were added: exemption from certain taxes and military service; distinctive clothes; celibacy as a required life-style. Those not ordained for sacramental service came to be described as "laity"—the inclusive New Testament word *laos* was now shrunk into a new, pejorative meaning. The vast proportion of believers were henceforward defined by what they *did not* do; thus was launched the long age of the baptized Christian as a passive religious consumer.

But not until the twelfth century did the barrier between clergy and laity harden into the shape we recognize today. During this turbulent century, newly asserted papal authority led to an explosion of an international Church bureaucracy. Ecclesiastical courts throughout Europe needed trained staff. The other great development of this century—the university—supplied the Church with "clerics" educated in theology and the new science of canon law. These officials served the Church in legal and administrative capacities rather than as community pastors. But this corps of Church civil servants were also ordained. In this fateful step, priesthood—sacramental leadership—was wed to clergy—the role of Church official.

During this same century celibacy became a legal requirement for ordination. The Lateran Council of 1139 restricted priesthood to unmarried men. For the first time in Christian memory the sacraments of matrimony and ordination were officially deemed incompatible. One legacy of this historical period is the adversarial relationship of clergy and laity. Priest-clerics were seen as ecclesiastical officials whose role was to protect the Church and its authority from "the laity." This latter term was now further narrowed to mean those princes and rich families who sought to influence the selection of bishops and the disposition of Church property. The new antagonism between clergy and laity found expression in the famous judgment of Pope Boniface VIII in 1296: "Lay persons have always been enemies of the clergy."

We revisit this shared history not to punish the past but to hold our history in a more responsible embrace. Recognizing the historical decisions by which our ancestors crafted a specific vision of Church leadership makes us participants in this process. We are those who must reaffirm and purify these decisions. In a season of fierce reevaluation and renewal, it is important to remember that we are living a success story. Christ's witness survives and even thrives after two thousand years. The historical decisions that have continually reshaped the Christian priesthood have been largely graceful. The success story continues, relying as always on the current community's courage and decisiveness.

Priestliness

The way through the crisis in the priesthood today is to rediscover the characteristics of priestliness. In the New Testament, "priest" (*sacerdos*) is not used to describe our leaders. The term first appears in the Letter to the Hebrews as a description of Jesus Christ. In the First Letter of Peter, all those who follow Jesus are entitled "a priestly people." The priestliness of Church leaders came from the Lord and community to whom they belonged.

What does it mean to be priestly? Jesus was not a priest in the sense of a cultic official, as was Zechariah, the father of John the Baptist (Luke 1). How, then, was his life "priestly"? Priestly behavior—in Jesus, his community, and the ordained leader—may be rooted in a witness to an abundance of grace. Jesus announced this abundance wherever he appeared: the availability of forgiveness, the possibility of healing, the access to a nourishment more satisfying than his hearers could imagine. The priestly witness of Jesus was an announcement of abundance. His listeners were, like us, accustomed to the many barriers to and restrictions on God's abundance. Being a foreigner, a tax collector, a woman, a sinner—all these severely jeopardized one's access to God's grace. Religious institutions, then as now, made it their business to control and limit the believer's access to grace. But Jesus insisted that grace was everywhere, overflowing the official channels, available in astonishing abundance.

Followers of Jesus become priestly when their lives witness to this same abundance. Communities that learn to forgive, to pursue justice, to nourish one another and all those in need: These groups are priestly. Their life in common announces an abundance of grace. And their testimony produces what they witness to: reconciliation, healing, and nourishment multiply among us.

Ordained leaders participate in this priestliness of the community and of Christ. Presbyters act in a priestly fashion when they remind the whole community of its calling to be priestly. Ordained leaders are not priests because others are not; they are priests in order to call others to their priestliness. The ordained ought not absorb all the priestliness in a community; their own sacramental ministry should reflect onto others, making priestliness more abundant. Current efforts to understand a "priesthood of the laity" are doomed because they remain embedded in the distinction between clergy and laity. Within such a dichotomy, the laity can only be ceded a rhetorical association with an attribute that belongs, essentially and uniquely, to the ordained leader. Only by letting go of the divisive categories of cleric and lay can we grasp again the energy and abundance of priestliness.

Clericalism

If priestliness is about the abundance of grace, clericalism is about its scarcity. Members of the clergy are Church officials who perform necessary services in the community of faith. These services may or may not include the ministry of presbyteral priesthood. When clerical officials build a privileged status for themselves, they succumb to the temptation of clericalism. As Francine Cardman and her colleagues describe in *The Renewal of Religious Life*, clericalism "is neither identical with nor a necessary consequence of priesthood, but a diminishment and distortion of it." The authors define clericalism as the "concern to promote the particular interests of the clergy and to protect the privileges and power that have traditionally been conceded to those in the clerical state." The manifestations of this attitude are "an authoritarian style in ministerial leadership, a rigidly hierarchical world view, a virtual identification of the holiness and grace of the Church with the clerical state." The authors are quick to add that laypersons fall into clericalism when their contributions to the Church are made in an elitist or dominating fashion.

Clericalism seeks to exclude the nonordained from leadership and to absorb the community's priestliness. By limiting access to formal leadership, clericalism makes grace scarce. Laypersons are told they cannot preach at a liturgy; this makes the good news scarce. Ordination is restricted to unmarried men; this guarantees that the sacraments will be in short supply. The most grievous offense of clericalism is its ambition to control the exuberant flow of the Spirit. Clericalism invents the category of laity as an adversary, as a threat to the abundance of its own authority. This attitude mimics a cultural vision of power as always in short supply: Your gain must be my loss; the preaching of an unordained person necessarily diminishes my authority. Clericalism creates scarcity.

But the priestly witness of Jesus testifies to abundance. Jesus' life proclaims an abundance of grace—wherever his followers act as a priestly people through their daily sacrifice of mercy, justice, and love. The priestliness of the faithful does not rob the leader of his own—unless we are still imbedded in a world of scarcity. As ordained ministers today move beyond the defense of clerical status and its anxiety about scarcity, they recover an abundance of priestliness in themselves and in others.

From today's vantage point we can trace the historical decisions through which our ancestors wrapped priesthood in the cloak of clericalism. A separate social caste, distinctive clothes, required celibacy: These are characteristics of clergy more than priesthood. For many centuries the ornate garment of the clergy protected and enhanced the priesthood. Today we are invited to unwrap this cloak that now constrains and stifles the priesthood. As we perform this delicate task, we begin to see the differences between genuine priestliness and clericalism.

A New Belonging

These upheavals in the Christian community jeopardize belonging. Ordained and unordained alike struggle to find a more satisfying and authentic way to participate in this holy gathering. Priests see their way through this purifying crisis as they discover new ways to belong.

Two slight but significant changes in our liturgical prayers illumine the leader's new position in the community. In the traditional final prayer of the Eucharist, the priest would pray: "Go in peace. The Mass is ended." As guardian of the sanctuary, the priest bids the people depart. But he will remain. This is where he lives. The sanctuary is his domain, just as the workplace and the family are the domain of the "laity." Leader and followers inhabit two different worlds.

Today in the community of faith one hears a slightly different departure prayer. The leader says: "*Let us go* in peace, to praise and serve the Lord." Let us go! We return together to our graced and wounded world. The leader acknowledges that he belongs with the community; he occupies no separate, sacred precinct. This is a new way of belonging.

A second familiar prayer is the blessing that the priest traditionally bestows on believers. "May God bless you in the name of the Father, the Son, and the Holy Spirit." Here, acting as God's spokesperson, the ordained leader dispenses God's own blessing. The implication is that, as priest, he has a special access to God, whose blessings he bestows. Such a possession makes the leader unique and sets him apart from the rest of us.

Often in the community of faith we hear another version of this blessing: "May God *bless us*, in the name of the Father, the Son, and the Holy Spirit." The priest still leads by publicly invoking God's blessing. But he is uttering a community's invocation of blessing instead of a leader's bestowal. And the leader stands with the assembly. May God bless *us*. The presbyteral leader awaits with others the blessing that only God can give.

In both these shifts in our prayer life, the priest remains leader—but he leads from a new location within the group. Neither elevated by his sacred status nor separated from a "secular laity," the priestly leader finds a more intimate and nourishing belonging in the community of faith.

Holy Week

In a crisis we struggle to name our loss. With God's grace we try to make sense of our distress—to reframe the pain. What holy image allows us to bear the losses we will sustain in the institutional purification that lies ahead?

In the decline in numbers, in the erosion of a once-clear identity, in the loss of a privileged status in the community, priesthood as we have known it is coming to an end. How can we face this cruel fact? The metaphor of Holy Week may support the Church in this crisis. This religious image gives our shared pain both a context and a direction. As Jesus prepared to go to Jerusalem the final time, his friends objected. The time is not right, Peter protested. Jesus, in one of his rare outbursts of anger, responded, "Get behind me, Satan!" (Mark 8:33). Approaching his death, Jesus experienced doubt and confusion. He resisted the abrupt and unfair end to his life; he begged the Father to take this cup of suffering from him. Finally, he gave himself to a rhythm he did not understand. With sorrow and regret he let go his plans and hopes and even his life, trusting in a power that was stronger than death.

The Catholic priesthood follows Jesus as it enters its Holy Week. Confusion and threat are in the air. Psalm 77 echoes through the Church: "This is the cause of my grief, that the ways of the Most High have changed." Despite denials and resistance, the Church is drawn along God's path. The institutional forms of priesthood, as we have known them over the past several hundred years, are moving toward death. The journey of Jesus rescues this mortal loss from absurdity.

Priesthood is on a painful journey of purification. As a continuing gift of God to the faith community, priesthood will not be lost. But it will be radically transformed. Its Good Friday will bring an end to the restriction imposed by clericalism: a priesthood limited to unmarried men; a priesthood that isolates the leader in privilege. Following Jesus into death, priesthood will be brought to new life.

By dying we come to life—this is Christianity's central conviction. Today it dawns on the Church that this pattern is true for priesthood itself. The Catholic community cannot flee the pain we feel at this approaching death, but we can learn to grieve our loss. As Americans we have been taught that grieving is a sign of weakness, a shameful submission to emotion and tears. Our culture instructs us to cut our losses, put our troubles behind us, and get on with life. These imperatives lead us to deny our distress and mask our mourning. But the Jewish-Christian tradition has left us another legacy about grieving: This is an honorable action and a necessary virtue.

When we grieve we acknowledge our pain and confusion before God. By holding up our loss to God we give our distress a voice: We transform our pain into prayer. Without this public acknowledgment, our pain remains mute, private, and hidden. Denying our distress can only lead us into depression and stagnation. This is not the way through a crisis, not the way of the cross.

Our colleague Gordon Myers summarizes his studies in group development: "If you want to keep a group from growing, keep it from grieving.'' Keep a community from facing its loss, from acknowledging the internal changes demanded if it is to grow. Distract the group with other tasks so it does not name its pain. Such a community—whether an individual parish or the universal Church—will consume its energy in useless projects or sink into a collective depression. Because it does not grieve, it will not grow.

Learning to Lament

Christians learn how to grieve from our ancient texts of lamentation. Job cries out: "Since I have lost all taste for life, I will give free rein to my complaints" (10:1). In the Book of Lamentations we read: "All you who pass this way, look and see: Is any sorrow like the sorrow that afflicts me?" (1:12). Grieving is a messy style of prayer, filled with anger, regret, and blame. It lacks the crispness and order that we Americans love but it is how we pray in Holy Week.

We might think that priests would be more versed than others in this style of prayer since they oversee the Holy Week liturgy. But many acknowledge the occupational hazard: Managing all the liturgies of this sacred season, the priest has no time for grieving. But as God calls us to a future that does not include all of our past, all of us must learn the disciplines of mourning. Theologian David Power summarizes the miracle that this prayer can work among us. "That which is remembered in grief is redeemed, made whole, renewed."

Today the paschal mystery embraces the Catholic priesthood. This is not bad news. As we face together the confusion and distress of this crisis, as we let go cherished ways of belonging, we offer up the purified lives in which God can craft the future of priestly service.

* * * * *

Additional Resources

Alexandre Faivre, in *The Emergence of the Laity in the Early Church* (Paulist, 1990), explores the original meanings of *laos* (people of God) and *kleros* (chosen one) and their reinterpretation as laity and clergy. English historian R. W. Southern provides a good overview of the historical changes in the Church in the twelfth century in *The Middle Ages: Western Society and the Church in the Middle Ages* (Penguin, 1970). Yves Congar traces the medieval meaning of "laity" in "Clercs et laïcs ou point de vue de la culture au moyen âge: 'laicus' = sans lettres," in his *Etudes d'ecclésiologie médiévale* (Variorum Reprints, 1983).

"In Solidarity and Service: Reflections on the Problem of Clericalism in the Church" by Francine Cardman and colleagues is a working paper prepared for the Conference of Major Superiors of Men and appeared in *Religious Life at the Crossroads*, ed. David Fleming (Paulist, 1985) 65–87.

Walter Brueggeman examines the dynamic of grief in the Jewish-Christian tradition in his excellent *The Prophetic Imagination* (Fortress, 1978). We discuss the dynamic of grieving as part of the Church's life these days in *The Promise of Partnership: Leadership and Ministry in an Adult Church* (Harper Collins, 1991). David Power's observation about the power of grieving to transform suffering is found in his "Household Church in the Coming Church," *Worship* 57 (May 1983) 254.

Accountability in Priesthood: Telling the Story of an Emerging Ministry

Evelyn Eaton Whitehead

> *"To want to be a presiding elder is to want to do a noble work."*
> 1 Timothy 3:1

Ministerial priesthood is a profession and more than a profession. For the priest himself, presbyteral ministry is part of the maturing of his baptismal call toward greater stewardship in the mission of Jesus. Acknowledging this personal experience of ministry, we are more keenly aware today that ministry is also a profession. Ministry as vocation shows us the personal face of priesthood; ministry as a profession invites us to look at priesthood's social face.

At the start we should acknowledge an American cultural ambivalence around the notion of a professional. The positive sense of the term is clear when we compliment someone for being professional. In this usage, to be a professional means to demonstrate wise judgment, expert performance, personal commitment to excellence, generous investment in the common good. But Americans are often suspicious of experts, wary of the power they wield and cynical about the motives that move them. So sometimes the word is more negative in nuance: The professional is one who is distant and uncaring, lacking genuine concern, hiding behind a role.

Whatever our current ambivalence, the notion of the professions has a long and distinguished history dating from the rise of the universities in the Middle Ages. Classically, the learned professions included medicine, law, and theology. Today the term embraces other occupations as well, especially in fields of human service such as education, counseling, and social work. As professions, each of these occupations (1) is an activity undertaken in the public realm (2) where practice is related to a particular body of knowledge and (3) in which practitioners are accountable to each other and to the profession as a whole. At its best, ministerial priesthood meets these criteria of a profession.

Public Practice

Priests play a public leadership role. Their ministry is a public practice, even when many of their activities—in pastoral counseling, spiritual direction, personal reconciliation—take place in private. Ordained ministers are public persons, their role recognized both within and beyond the faith community they serve. The civic community acknowledges religious ministry (when, for example, a prominent religious leader is asked to serve on a city task force dealing with interracial justice or housing for the homeless) and often recognizes the contribution of the minister's service (when, for example, the chaplain's position at a community hospital is subsidized by public funds or when local pastors are called to the scene of a natural disaster to comfort those affected), even when many citizens do not share the minister's beliefs.

Theory and Practice

When pastoral practice flows from an informed appreciation of Scripture and is rooted in theological reflection, ministerial priesthood meets the second characteristic of a profession. In the United States through the first half of this century, mainline Protestant denominations kept alive the notion of the theologian-pastor. Many Catholic priests ordained before Vatican II, however, recall completing their seminary education convinced that—whatever else might be said of their place in the Church—they were clearly not theologians. Today we acknowledge "pastoral theologian" as part of the job description of the ministerial priesthood. The best current seminary education introduces students not only to the history of theology and the works of major theologians but to the process of theological reflection. And effective pastoral ministers make this process their own by learning to forge connections between the vital tradition of Christian belief and the hopes and struggles of the Church today. Increasingly, priests recognize continuing pastoral education as both their right and their responsibility. Without the nourishment of ongoing theological study, both priestly spirituality and presbyteral ministry suffer.

Professional Accountability

Internal accountability is a hallmark of the professions. While regarded as public practice, the professions traditionally have been exempt from public regulation. A moral pledge—that the profession would regulate itself—reassured the large community that no social watchdog was required. Society could count on professional practitioners to hold themselves and one another accountable for safeguarding society's interests. Recent events in American life—the Watergate political scandal, the perceived increase in medical malpractice, the growing strength of the consumer advocacy movement—have called this assumption into question. Today the American Medical Association, the American Bar Association, and similar professional organizations strenuously resist attempts by outsiders, whether government agencies or consumer groups, to establish policies or performance criteria for their practitioners. In their lobbying efforts these associations often appeal to the implicit ethical promise of every profession—that society is safe in its hands.

The American public, troubled by increasing professional malpractice and angered by escalating professional fees, is less likely to accept this promise at face value today. The ethical commitment of professionals is now something to be demonstrated rather than simply assumed. The priesthood, too, has fallen under this public suspicion. In many places charges of fiscal misconduct and sexual abuse, many of them founded in fact, have undermined the Catholic community's confidence in its institutional leaders. Nevertheless, the expectation of personal accountability remains integral to an understanding of the professions.

Accountability in Ministry

Professional accountability is part of presbyteral ministry today. Canon law, for example, defines the range of the diocesan priest's responsibility to the local Ordinary, the parish council, and other ecclesiastical bodies. Diocesan personnel policy and ministry job descriptions often describe these responsibilities in greater detail. These formal documents generally state the explicit requirements of *juridical* accountability, specifying when and to whom the priest must give a justifying report of his ministerial practice. True, in many places these procedures of accountability are not yet fully functioning. For example, some priest personnel boards invoke statutes of juridical accountability only in problem cases; diocesan attorneys use them to justify quick action against a priest whose behavior might leave the diocese at risk of a civil lawsuit. But in the decades ahead, these ordinary practices of juridical accountability are likely to become an expected and appreciated part of Church organizational life.

But the accountability that interests us here goes beyond the legal parameters of this juridical sense. A deeper "accountability" characterizes ministry. Within the body of Christ, those who minister must be able to "render an account" of God's grace active in their own lives. Presbyteral ministers must be able to "tell the story" of their servant leadership in the community of faith.

Three factors in contemporary ministry heighten the need for priests to be able to "tell the story" of their own emerging vocation. These are (1) diverse understandings of the priesthood, (2) increased collaboration between priests and others in ministry, and (3) purifications of the institution of priesthood itself.

Diverse Understandings of Priesthood

In the Church of the 1940s and 1950s, Catholics shared a broad consensus about our religious leaders and their role among us. Priests—and the rest of us—knew what was expected of them. The deep respect and ready obedience they inspired was rooted in a generally accepted theology of priesthood. Clergy and laity alike understood the priest to be an essential mediator of God's grace, through the sacraments (to which the priest alone had direct access) and through the otherness of his life as a sacred person. The priest was the primary, even exclusive, minister to the spiritual needs of the Catholic community. His soul marked with the indelible character of the sacrament of holy orders, the priest was essentially different from others in the community. Whatever the limits of his personal ability or even his moral rectitude, the priest was "another Christ."

The experience of the Catholic community over the past three decades has called this theological understanding into question. Many priests today find the conventional definitions of priesthood at odds with their own experience. But efforts to express a post–Vatican II understanding of ordained ministry are still in the early stages. As yet, no clear or widely convincing reformulation replaces the consensus that has been lost.

What is the role of the priest? Theologians, bishops, and priests themselves differ widely in their response. Is the priest a nurturing parent of the children of God, devoted to direct care for the spiritual needs of the laity? Or a responsible steward in an adult community of faith, called to facilitate and coordinate the multiple ministries of the people of God? Should the pastor stand as prophetic herald of the reign of God, challenging the congregation to assume greater responsibility for peace and justice? Or does he stand as wounded healer in our midst, witnessing to God's tender mercy toward those broken by personal pain and loss?

Plural theologies of priesthood lead to diverse expectations. The priest needs to articulate his own sense of what his priesthood means and what his ministerial responsibilities are, lest he be simply a victim of other people's demands.

Increasing Collaboration in Ministry

This is a season of collaboration in ministry. Former distinctions, which once accurately described the community of faith and divided our respective areas of concern, no longer serve us well. In ministry today, people are crossing over the boundaries that used to set clergy apart from laity, women apart from men, professionals apart from those who volunteered their services. Many factors are part of this increasing interdependence. Decreasing numbers of priests bring increasing numbers of experienced women religious and well-trained laymen and laywomen into roles once seen exclusively as priestly ministry. Contemporary ecclesiology stresses that ministry, a gift of the Spirit to the whole Church, is not meant to be done alone. Many priests know from personal experience the benefits of partnership in ministry: Joint action can accomplish what individual effort cannot. And beyond increased effectiveness, collaboration offers mutual support and encouragement in the midst of the demanding and often difficult work of religious leadership.

Ministry today is increasingly interdependent. Teamwork, effective cooperation, shared decision making—these are the hope and substance of much that is best in contemporary pastoral life. This interdependence has many benefits but collaboration has demands as well. Frequently, partners in collaborative ministry have to coordinate their work schedules or negotiate the use of limited resources—the parish hall or the activities budget or the list of eager parish volunteers. To work together in ministry, colleagues must be able to talk about what they need from one another at this practical level.

But collaborative ministry often demands a deeper discussion as well. Those working closely together in ministry today—priests and laity, women and men, professionals and volunteers—often find that their pastoral activities call into question some of the roles and rules of the established organizational arrangement. As colleagues struggle with the practical details of "who does what around here," questions of leadership and authority emerge; issues of initiative and influence arise. Those who work together must be able to speak to one another—directly and without manipulation—about these concerns.

Collaboration requires discussion and negotiation. A priest out of touch with his own story, unaware of the charisms and limits of his personal contribution, finds this discussion threatening. Without the flexibility that comes from self-awareness, any questioning of "the way we usually do things around here" seems like a personal attack on his leadership. In the community of faith today, the priest no longer takes up all the space of ministry. To be effective in this new collaborative setting, a priest must be able to clarify—with and for his ministry colleagues—the precise scope of his own work and how this service connects with the vocations and ministries of others in the community of faith. This discussion does not demand the self-disclosure of deep personal friendship, but it does require that the priest be able to share his vision, to explain his ideas, to say how he thinks and how he feels about issues that touch on the ministry he shares with others.

Purification of Priesthood

In this season of purification, as James Whitehead notes in his chapter in this volume, former definitions of priesthood fall away. Discrepancy widens between these earlier formulations and the actual vocation of priests today. Stripped of these theological supports, many priests feel vulnerable and exposed. But in the midst of their personal crises, some of these men sense God crafting a renewed priesthood. "Who am I as presbyter? What is my role in the community?" Answers to these questions will not arise magically. The shape of a renewed priesthood will emerge, in part, from the reliable witness of priests today telling the story of their own vocation.

In a period of profound change, then, accountability serves not only the priest's personal survival. As the Church struggles to understand the core of contemporary priesthood, theology lags behind the life experience of many priests. This experience is a key source of information—a genuinely theological source—about the direction in which the Spirit moves. The faith community needs priests reflective enough to attend to what God is doing in their lives and bold enough to tell this story. In this, they show the Church God's future.

Requirements of Accountability

To render an account of his ministry requires, first, that a priest knows what he is doing and, second, that he can communicate what he is doing.

I Know What I Am Doing

Being accountable helps the priest discern his particular strengths for service and befriend his genuine limitations. Lacking this clarity, many priests find it difficult to specify their ministry, to determine the focus of their particular contribution to the coming of God's reign. But an unspecified sense of personal vocation leaves priests victim to demands that they live up to heroic expectations—their own or other people's.

The heroic image casts leaders as larger than life. The priest, as hero, is a man for others—universally available, abundantly talented, clairvoyantly wise, able to give without counting the cost, willing to serve without asking anything in return. Many priests hold themselves accountable to that standard. When their experience shows them to be less than all this, priests often respond by judging *themselves* to be inadequate, rather than questioning the heroic role.

A priest aware of his personal talents and wounds is more effective in ministry and more open to collaboration. Other people in ministry—women, laypeople—are less a threat, since his own ministry is rooted more firmly in personal charism than in unreal expectations. "What he does" flows out of "who he is" rather than the other way around.

Confidence is thus a second benefit of self-awareness. The conviction that "I do some things well" buoys the minister. He may not "do well" all the things he has to do on a day-to-day basis; few priests find themselves in ministry settings that so perfectly match their talents. But "account-ability" demands knowing what one does well. Rendering an account of God's grace means, in part, being able to tell the success story of one's vocation. And success stories build self-confidence.

If ministerial clarity and vocational confidence are goals of accountability, pastoral evaluation is the means. Knowing what one is doing demands reflection on one's work, not just on motives but on actual performance and its real effects.

By evaluation we mean a systematic effort to assess one's pastoral activities in order to understand, to appreciate, and to improve. *To understand:* Over the course of a few years, or even several months, the substance of a priest's work may change, even if he remains in the same official position. Without taking time on a regular basis to assess what he is actually doing, a priest may lose touch with the direction and scope of his own ministry. *To appreciate:* With presbyteral ministry in flux, the criteria for judging its value become blurred. Many priests are left without much sense of the weight and worth of what they do. Evaluation helps us value what we do by clarifying our own values. Professional evaluation begins in the process of discovering one's own criteria for "a job well done." When properly undertaken, the first fruit of a regular program of self-assessment is a more profound appreciation of the worth of one's own efforts. *To improve:* Reflecting on pastoral practice can show a priest where and how he wants to improve. Moving beyond a vague uneasiness that "things are not going well," he can identify places in his ministry where he is stretched beyond his ability or where his current skills fall short. This concrete information can guide his decisions of what to do next, whether this signals a change in ministry setting, a program of pastoral study, or a commitment to personal counseling.

But for all its acknowledged benefits, evaluation remains a troublesome notion for many in ministry. Perfectionism is a personal wound that many of us carry. Priests burdened by perfectionism hold unrealistic personal goals; anything less than complete accomplishment is interpreted as failure. For the perfectionist, evaluation looms as an occasion of shame: "Here I will be found out." In fact, as many counselors recognize, a regular program of evaluation can be an ascetical practice helping to heal the addiction to perfection. With a sensitive mentor or ministry supervisor, a priest can learn to set personal goals more expressive of his own values and more reflective of his real talents. Especially, he can find support in his efforts to ease up on himself.

The institutional shadow of paternalism further complicates evaluation. As a pattern of authority, paternalism suggests that someone else knows what is best for us, what is properly expected of us. Paternalistic authority often uses punitive patterns of evaluation to reestablish control, belittling those whose behaviors do not comply with institutional norms.

The increasing expectation that a community of faith should participate in the evaluation of its leaders raises more complications. With little historical memory and few tested tools of mutual accountability, communities often stumble in their initial efforts to provide honest feedback to their religious leaders. Lacking techniques that clearly embody the spirit of the gospel, religious groups often adopt evaluation strategies in use elsewhere (in business or politics or civil service). Recent experience shows that the religious leader is especially vulnerable when these strategies are used uncritically in religious groups. In such settings, "pastoral evaluation" becomes a code word for "get the pastor."

Several safeguards help insure that evaluation serves— rather than undermines—genuine accountability. Being judged by other people's norms expectably puts people on the defensive. Most importantly, then, the priest himself should be involved in deciding the criteria that will be used to assess his ministry. Secondly, these criteria should focus not on the priest's motives or personality, but on his observable behavior: What he *does* is the appropriate focus of ministry evaluation.

Finally, care should be given to the proper context for pastoral evaluation. Evaluation supports a priest's deeper "account-ability" only if he is not left vulnerable. Self-scrutiny is risky business; trust makes that risk reasonable. Support and confidentiality, then, are essential to any evaluation process. Vulnerability also raises the issue of timing, reminding us that communal evaluation serves best in unheated times. For example, when a parish is already in the midst of crisis, evaluating the pastor easily falls into scapegoating—an attempt to assign blame for the community's distress. In contrast, when the priest requests feedback at a time that makes sense to him (when, for example, he feels he is going stale in his current work or when he wants an outside view of an issue or problem he faces), evaluation can be a moment of grace for the priest and for the community as well.

I Am Able to Say What I Am Doing

Presbyteral ministry, as we have noted above, is a public practice. Every priest is engaged with several "publics"— the faith community in which he serves, the larger civic community, his immediate ministry colleagues, the brotherhood of diocesan priests or the religious congregation, the network of Church officials within the diocese and beyond. In different ways and for a range of reasons, priests today find themselves accountable to these different groups. Priests need to—or want to—tell the story of their ministry, recognizing that their different audiences speak different languages. Genuine accountability, then, requires that priests can express their emerging vocation in a range of vocabularies. The pastor shares his vision of the parish with members of the parish council; to the priests in his faith-sharing group he confides his uneasiness with being middle-aged and his concern about growing older; at a vicariate meeting he draws on his own pastoral experience to lobby for a reformulation of the diocesan guidelines for team ministry. In each of these settings he "renders an account," tells something of the story of his own vocation, even though the style and substance of his account may be quite different in each case.

To be accountable, priests need to feel comfortable in the diverse vocabularies of their profession. Scripture supplies the basic text of the Christian story; the priest's account of his own vocation draws power from the biblical language of covenant and prophecy, nourishment and reconciliation, life through death. Theology is the official language in many parts of the ecclesial community; in these settings, a priest's personal story will carry weight only if it can be expressed in cogent theological terms. In some ecclesiastical circles, canon law is the dominant language; to have one's story understood means to cast it in canonical categories. Elsewhere in the faith community, the story finds its deepest expression in gospel metaphors—sower and seed, the pearl of great price, the way of the cross. Using these metaphors in homilies, pastoral counseling, and public prayer, the priest can share his own faith experience, giving an account of God's grace that is within him in ways that strengthen others on the journey.

Support for Accountability

Genuine accountability does not come easy. Telling the story of one's own vocation requires courage, because not everyone will applaud and not everyone will agree. Telling one's story also requires a forum for the conversation, a setting in which genuine interest and demonstrated trust invite an honest discussion. So, especially in this season of transformation for the institution of priesthood, priests need to find and build strong networks of support.

At the core of an effective support network are significant personal relationships—the affection of loved ones, the understanding of trusted confidants, the sure devotion of close friends. Close relationships like these, often nourished in priests' support groups, bless the lives of many priests today, strengthening their resolve on the journey of faith. Other relationships offer other kinds of support. In the midst of the confusions of institutional change, some priests experience the sense of solidarity that comes from linking their lives with people who share their values—in small faith communities, in social-justice networks, in recovery groups. Others know they can count on ministry colleagues—fellow priests, lay ministers and vowed religious, clergy of other faith traditions—who recognize their competence and appreciate their skills. In this season of institutional change, three additional relationships support presbyteral accountability.

Ministry Supervisor

Twenty years ago James Gill, Jesuit psychiatrist and founder of the influential spirituality journal *Human Develop-*

ment, wrote: "I know of no profession or career where there is a more intimate link between a person's technical competence and the development of his own personality than exists in the priesthood. . . . I know of no better way to help priests grow professionally than to provide them a competent supervisor or mentor who will evaluate with them their potential, their performance, and the effectiveness of their work, keeping in mind the man's talents, goals, motives, attitudes, and other personality factors."

Gill's conviction is shared widely today among those committed to the initial and ongoing formation of priests. More important still, increasing numbers of priests themselves affirm the value of the supervisory relationship. Through participation in seminary field education sequences, clinical pastoral education courses, or doctor of ministry programs, many priests have worked closely with a pastoral supervisor. Learning the benefits of examining their work in the presence of such an experienced and supportive colleague, a number of priests are reluctant to lose supervision when the formal program comes to an end. Upon returning to full-time ministry, some priests continue regular contact with an earlier supervisor; others are successful in developing a new supervisory relationship. Sometimes priests experienced in ministry commit themselves to mutual supervision: Coming together on a regular basis, these men take turns presenting issues of pastoral concern, critique one another's pastoral practice, and help one another generate alternative strategies for action. Both improved ministry and enhanced confidence result.

Spiritual Companion

Discerning the movement of one's vocation demands times of solitude, but fidelity to this movement is seldom sustained alone. Wayne Fehr, director of spiritual care at Saint Barnabas Center in Wisconsin, a treatment facility for religious and clergy, notes one of the most dangerous—and paradoxical—occupational hazards of the minister's role: "Few clergy have had the occasion or willingness to reveal to anyone else the true state of their spiritual life. They often lack the kind of trusted friend who could understand their struggles of faith. Moreover, their role of authority figure often makes it nearly impossible to disclose any of their own limitations or failures, especially in the area of spirituality."

Many priests today recognize that their own spiritual life cannot be left to chance. Attention must be paid, time must be spent, priority must be given to the daily disciplines of open presence to God, personal prayer, honest self-awareness, and thanksgiving. For most of us, this religious awareness is sustained best by the committed companionship of a spiritual guide or soul friend. "Going it alone," difficult in many aspects of professional ministry these days, is especially risky on the spiritual journey.

Political Allies

A religious institution, like all institutions, runs on both procedures and politics. Some holy priests are gifted with native political instincts. But many people drawn to ministry find politics, especially Church politics, somehow unseemly. For those of us who characteristically disdain organizational politics, developing institutional allies can be an unnerving asceticism.

But political allies are important to presbyteral accountability today. In time of organizational crisis, when institutional purification is needed and public dissent is risky, telling the truth can become a political act. To tell the story of one's own ministry, to help reveal the shape of an emerging priesthood, may entail political risk. Political allies, that is, people familiar with the organizational structure and conscious of the formal and informal channels of influence, can support one's "account-ability." Our political allies need not be our close friends; they need not always agree with us or support our agenda for reform. But, savvy about the system and sensitive to the way it responds, political allies can alert us to the likely ramifications of our actions. By advising on questions of strategy and pointing out some of the dangers ahead of time, political allies can provide essential support to a priest's efforts to work through complex institutional issues surrounding his ministry and to discern his own faithful, if prophetic, response.

A Place to Start

Developing the disciplines of personal accountability can start many ways. A review of one's current experience is often a good place to begin. I offer here a simple reflective tool to guide such a review. And to the priests of today and tomorrow who stand with and within the Church, I offer my gratitude and respect.

Exploring Ministerial Accountability

A. Who are my "publics"?
    —those to whom I *need* to tell the story of my ministry
    —those to whom I *want* to tell the story of my ministry

B. With which of these publics have I been successful in telling my story? What factors (in me, in them, in the setting) have contributed to this success?

C. With which of my "publics" do I have difficulty in sharing the story of my ministry? Why does this seem to be the case; what are the factors (in me, in them, in the situation) that complicate the dialogue?

D. What can I do about it? How can I be more genuinely "accountable" in these diverse settings of my ministry?

E. Where can I find support for my accountability? Identify those people whose honesty, affection, challenge, and good sense help me to be faithful to the emerging story of my own vocation.

* * * * *

Additional Resources

Donald A. Schon, a respected professor of social psychology and organizational development at the Massachusetts Institute of Technology, explores the shape of accountability in *The Reflective Practitioner: How Professionals Think in Action* (New York: Basic Books, 1983). Robert N. Bellah and William M. Sullivan take up questions of the religious professional in "The Professions and the Common Good: Vocation/Profession/Career," *Religion & Intellectual Life*, vol. 4, no. 3 (Spring 1987) 7–20; in the same issue, see also Steven Murphy, "Resistance in the Professions," 71–80.

The Alban Institute, a mainline Protestant think-tank devoted to issues of congregational life, has long been engaged in the issue of clergy accountability and evaluation; see, for example, Lored Mead's paper, "Evaluation: Of, by, for, and to the Clergy," as well as the continuing consideration of related themes in the Institute's newsletter, *Action Information*. For membership and publication information, contact Alban Institute, 4125 Nebraska Avenue NW, Washington, DC 20016. See also the study document, *Excellence in Ministry: The Personal and Professional Needs of the Clergy*, and the newsletter of the Cornerstone Project, entitled Update, designed to support and strengthen the ordained leadership of the Episcopal Church; both are available through The Episcopal Church Foundation, 815 Second Avenue, New York, NY 10017.

James Gill's comment on ministry supervision is found on page 143 in his "Personal Accountability and the Priest," *Chicago Studies*, vol. 12, no. 2 (Summer 1973) 129–154. Wayne Fehr discusses "The Spiritual Assessment of Clergy in Crisis" in *Action Information*, vol. 16, no. 4 (July/August 1990) 6–8; quote is from page 8.

Our discussion of priesthood as part of an emerging network of ministerial leadership continues in James D. Whitehead and Evelyn Eaton Whitehead, *The Promise of Partnership: Leadership and Ministry in an Adult Church* (San Francisco: Harper Collins, 1991).

The Spirituality of the Diocesan Priest

Donald B. Cozzens

I write this chapter as a fifty-year-old priest observing the silver jubilee of his ordination and the just past twenty-fifth anniversary of the close of the Second Vatican Council. The past quarter century has taken many surprising turns, turns my classmates and I never anticipated. The tides of culture, both life giving and destructive, have changed the coastlines of society and Church. In and through these changes, God's Spirit has brought about a breathtaking reshaping of the ecclesiastical order, which has occasioned significant and often dramatic breakthroughs in our theological understanding of the Church itself, the role of the laity, the episcopacy, and, in particular, the priesthood.

This reshaping of the ecclesiastical order has prompted new investigations into the nature and identity of the ministerial priesthood. In the midst of, and in spite of, significant theological research (see David Power's chapter on the theology of the priesthood), priests ministering in the postconciliar era find themselves in the hold of a tenacious identity crisis. Aware of the challenge to grapple with a deeper and richer theology of priesthood and painfully conscious of the concomitant issue of identity, the priest of the 1990s senses an urgent need to be grounded in a mature and vital spirituality—a spirituality that emerges out of his lived experience of being priest and pastor.

Until recently, the diocesan priest's spirituality was eclectic, an amalgam of quasi-monastic Jesuit, Dominican, and Franciscan spiritualities often filtered through Sulpician and Irish approaches to the spiritual life. Alongside these traditions, a contemplative strain, mostly Cistercian and Carmelite in character, is observable in the spiritual lives of a growing number of diocesan priests. Thomas O'Meara writes: "The diocesan priest for long has had, at best, spiritualities which were derivative: that of the Benedictine monks, of the Jesuits, of the clerics regular. Church authorities are right to be concerned over the spirituality . . . of the priest and seminarian."[1] While enriched by these various spiritual traditions and indeed indebted to them, the diocesan priest concedes that they have grown out of charisms not necessarily his own. In spite of emerging theologies of priesthood not yet fully articulated and the related issue of his identity, the diocesan priest continues to search for a spirituality properly his own. This chapter is a contribution toward the emerging spirituality of the diocesan priest.

* * * * *

More than a few veteran observers of the Church insist that the most pressing issue facing Catholicism today is the quality of its priestly leadership. This issue, they claim, is of greater significance than the role of women in ministry, the ordination of married individuals, obligatory celibacy, or the election of bishops. No matter how one ranks the quality of priestly leadership on any scale of Church priorities, it is clearly a matter of concern for the vitality of the Church in whatever age the Church finds itself. Implicit in any discussion of the quality of priestly ministry is the authenticity and maturity of the priest's spirituality. It remains the fundamental issue undergirding his preaching, presiding, pastoral care, facilitating, and administering. While pastoral skills can be taught, they remain techniques unless rooted in a vibrant spiritual life. It is not surprising, then, that considerable attention has been given to the spiritual life of the priest throughout the Church's history. This is particularly true since the Second Vatican Council. Eight years after the council's close, The United States Catholic Conference published *The Spiritual Renewal of the American Priesthood*, edited by Ernest E. Larkin and Gerard T. Broccolo, a publication following closely upon the psychological, sociological, and historical studies of the priesthood commissioned and funded by the American bishops. In 1977 the Bishops' Committee on Priestly Life and Ministry published *As One Who Serves*. Each of these documents treated either directly or indirectly the spirituality of the priest in the United States. Recent years have seen the publication of *Reflections on the Morale of Priests* by the Bishops' Committee on Priestly Life and Ministry of the National Conference of Catholic Bishops and Robert M. Schwartz's *Servant Leaders of the People of God: An Ecclesial Spirituality for American Priests.* These important works, along with numerous other books and articles on the American priesthood, point to an emerging spirituality for the American priest and, in particular, the American diocesan priest.

Spirituality, in its broadest context, refers to the human experience of being connected, both in reality and mystery, to that which is ultimate.[2] We may speak of Christian spirituality as "the living out in experience, throughout the whole course of our lives, of the death-resurrection of Christ that we have been caught up into by baptism."[3] These understandings of spirituality take us beyond the notion that spirituality is reducible to holiness, though holiness remains an essential and fundamental component of the spiritual life. We have come to understand spirituality as encompassing the whole of one's life in relationship to that which is ultimate. In the life of the Christian, it is the concrete experience of grace and healing in the paschal mystery, the daily dying and rising, the daily experience of communion and alienation, of virtue and sin, that constitute our redeemed lives in Christ. Spirituality may be thought of as the Christian's existential experience of the mystery of grace and his or her attempt to reflect upon that mystery and to name it. Spirituality, then, appears as the context or environment that reveals one's life as graced relationship to God and others in Christ and the Holy Spirit. Our discussion, then, of the spirituality of the diocesan priest is an examination of the specific context and environment that constitute his life and unfold, through his decisions and commitments, lifestyle, and ministry, his transformation in the death and resurrection of Christ.

Three Preliminary Issues

Three issues have appeared on the horizon of the diocesan priest's life that have shaken his confidence and challenged his sense of self. They have, at the same time, like a strong wind buffeting a small boat, disrupted his spiritual orientation. I am referring to the issues of identity, intimacy, and integrity. Each requires some discussion before we can address our central concern, the spirituality of the diocesan priest.

Identity

While some priests deny concern about their priestly identity, most concede that this issue hangs over their heads like a storm cloud, robbing them of the confidence they once knew and rendering them awkward and self-conscious in certain parish and social situations. Postconciliar priests know of the competing theologies of priesthood: those grounded in the classical approach, which emphasize the ontological character of priests, and those influenced by the historical method, which place the ministerial priesthood in the context of the Church's call, rooted in baptism, to be a priestly people. When they gather with their brother priests, they are able to discern with little difficulty more or less where each man stands on this issue. It surfaces in their remarks and attitudes about ministry and women and the issues that affect their lives. They are aware of the attention Vatican II gave to the episcopacy and diaconate, in contrast to the limited treatment accorded to the ministerial priesthood. For the most part, they have greeted enthusiastically the theological developments that have expanded the role of the laity and situated the origin of all ministries in baptism. While a renewed theology of priesthood is emerging, it has been held in careful check by Vatican authorities. It appears that a contemporary theology of priesthood would necessarily raise certain controversial issues such as the ministerial use of inactive and laicized priests, a married clergy, and the role of women in ministry. A number of priests know that the theological study of the American priesthood commissioned by the National Conference of Catholic Bishops in the late 1960s (along with the sociological, psychological, and historical studies) was rejected by the bishops in spite of the sound work done by the writing team. The impression persists that the theological study posed a threat to the time-honored traditions of obligatory celibacy and an all male priesthood.

Nevertheless, priests are greatly encouraged by the candor of the 1988 document issued by the Bishops' Committee on Priestly Life and Ministry, *Reflections on the Morale of Priests*. Among the concerns they identify as having a negative impact on the morale of priests is that of "differing perceived ecclesiologies." These different ecclesiologies, as we have noted, generate different theologies of ministry and priesthood, which in turn cloud the issue of presbyteral identity. The document on morale quotes an observation made in the 1982 publication *The Priest and Stress* that underscores the impact of different and competing ecclesiologies. "The priestly profession is one that must work within an ecclesial community that is polarized. Sometimes vastly differing notions of faith, ecclesiology, law and ministry are to be found within the same rectory. This is a cause of tension, especially when the individuals must not only work together but share common living arrangements. . . . When a mentality of self-righteousness on either end of the theological spectrum exists, a debilitating wear on the person whose responsibility it is to try to forge some common understanding results."[4]

Another development obfuscating the identity of the priest is the expansion of ministries called for by the Second Vatican Council and explicated in Thomas O'Meara's 1983 study, *Theology of Ministry*.[5] For most priests ordained prior to or shortly after the council, ministry meant priestly ministry. The explosion of ministries described by O'Meara has changed all that. While most priests welcome the new and expanding ministries gracing our Church, they experience a need to reflect upon their own priestly ministry, their relationship to the new ministries, and the concomitant call to collaboration. Those who work with ordained ministers know that their response to the expansion of ministries in the Church is anything but consistent. Some have readily adjusted to their colleagues in ministry while others have felt threatened and anxious. There is no doubt that the priest's identity has been dramatically called into question by these new ministries. O'Meara writes: "Many challenges to present and future priests come from an expanding and diverse ministry. Since Vatican II, the identity of the priest has become more active than static, more diaconal than sacral, more diverse than routine, more communal than solitary and monastic. . . . Today priestly identity comes not only from sacramental leadership but from communal and ministerial leadership."[6]

Commenting on the studies of the priesthood commissioned by the American bishops and published in the early 1970s, Andrew Greeley suggests that there has been "a loss of nerve, a loss of discipline, a loss of sense of identity in the priesthood."[7] That a loss of nerve and identity is common in today's priesthood is supported by the low job satisfaction found among associate pastors and the reluctance of priests to recruit candidates for seminary training.[8] The causes of this apparent loss of nerve and identity, I believe, go beyond our differing theologies of priesthood and the expanding ministries of our Church. Alongside these ecclesial phenomena, the secular nature of our society questions the meaning and relevancy of religion in general and celibate priesthood in particular. In a secular environment priests are regularly perceived as marginal figures who are considered briefly and with amused detachment. The message is patronizingly clear: While society still requires that a certain respect be shown the clergy, it is doctors and lawyers, business persons and politicians, scientists and bankers, who play the important roles. The peripheral role of the priest has apparently dampened his spirit and eroded his confidence. Yet Greeley and others report that priests remain enormously important to Catholics in general as well as to society as a whole.[9]

The very secularity of much of American life has led to a crisis in meaning and to the loss of a sense of mystery and reverence—all issues of spirituality. It can be argued that never before has the role of the priest, rabbi, and minister been more urgently needed in our society than it is at the present time. While poets and novelists also address the questions of meaning and mystery, priests, in particular, should be at home here. Unfortunately, many are not. A good number of priests appear to be in retreat, striking the pose of either the reactionary legalist and moralist or of the nondirective therapist championing a pseudo liberalism and relativism that makes sincerity the only criterion for ethical behavior. Have they somehow lost touch with the passion of the gospel, with its mystery, paradox, and meaning? To the extent that this is true in some priests, they, indeed, have lost their nerve. The reclaiming of the priest's nerve, that is, his sense of mission, as well as the discovery of his postconciliar identity, are issues intimately associated with a spirituality properly his own.

Intimacy

Perhaps no turn of phrase has more aptly and succinctly captured the spirit of our age than the title of Philip Rieff's book, *The Triumph of the Therapeutic*.[10] While the extent of therapy's triumph may be disputed, it is clear that it has had its day. It is easy to observe the influence of the therapeutic in our schools, courtrooms, and churches. Our fascination with the insights of contemporary psychology, I believe, has been generally beneficial. The therapeutic mentality has fostered healing for the broken and wounded and encouraged more creative and fulfilling life-styles. Not only has it had a profound impact upon education, law, and religion but also upon family life and management theory; indeed, upon almost every aspect of society. Psychology and the social sciences in general rightly take credit for their contribution to the holistic emphasis seen in medicine, psychotherapy, and spirituality. Developmental psychologists, in identifying the stages we ordinarily pass through in our psychosexual, ethical, and faith lives, have furthered our understanding of the complexity of human and spiritual growth. On the other hand, the downside of the triumph of the therapeutic has led some to view spirituality as but another means to personal fulfillment. The reality of grace, the profound relational character of spirituality, the centrality of ritual and symbol, are easily dismissed or overlooked when spirituality suffers such a reduction.

I believe that the human soul has two basic longings: It longs for intimacy and for transcendence. So strong is its hunger for these two realities that failing to find authentic intimacy and transcendence, the soul will turn to pseudo or plastic forms. For example, often what motivates individuals to pursue promiscuous sexual encounters is the unrequited hunger for intimacy. Sexuality, being a major paradigm for union, is readily confused with authentic intimacy. If authentic experiences of transcendence go unmet, pseudo states of transcendence are brought on by the use, and often abuse, of alcohol and other chemicals. Individuals graced with a vital spiritual life regularly experience intimacy and transcendence in their lives. Priests, through their life of prayer and service, their almost daily contact with ritual and symbol, readily meet their souls' hunger for transcendence. Intimacy, for the celibate priest, is another matter. Failure to develop authentic celibate relationships of intimacy has led both to spiritual and vocational crises in the lives of countless priests.

Authentic human intimacy is a hallmark of the mature and healthy adult. The capacity for mature and honest relationships is also critical for a sound and mature spiritual life.[11] While the issue of intimacy is problematic for society as a whole, it appears to be especially troublesome for priests. The psychological and sociological studies of the American priesthood commissioned by the National Conference of Catholic Bishops and published in the early 1970s found that priests were not as mature as their comparably educated male counterparts. "The ordinary men who are American priests are bright, able and dedicated. A large number of them are underdeveloped as persons with a consequent lack of fully realized religious and human values. . . . They could be far more effective personally and professionally if they were helped to achieve greater human and religious maturity."[12] Though these studies are now dated, there is no evidence to suggest that their findings do not hold true today. To the extent that priests tend to be emotionally underdeveloped and immature, the issue of intimacy will remain problematic to both their spiritual and personal lives.

There are large numbers of priests whose legitimate intimacy needs remain unknown to them. Aware that something is missing and often unable to name that which is missing, they wrestle with their souls' restlessness and discomfort. Prayer is intensified, spiritual directors are consulted, retreats are made—but the vague yet persistent feeling that something is missing disturbs their peace of soul. Whenever this state of soul exists, the celibacy issue looms large. What is missing is judged to be wife and children and the archetypal comforts of family and home. While this may indeed be the case for a good number of priests, for many others it is more an issue of a fundamental human need not being met: the need for intimacy. Individuals with a capacity for intimacy are mature adults who have come to accept both their goodness and their limitations. They have both a deep sense of their own self-worth rooted in the pervading presence and mystery of God's grace and a quiet confidence in their abilities and achievements. They possess both the courage and skill to make appropriate self-disclosure, without which intimacy remains impossible. This capacity for authentic intimacy shapes the context and influences the depth of an individual's spiritual life. Priests who have acknowledged and addressed their intimacy needs as mature, celibate men enjoy a spiritual life quite different in tone and texture from that of their brothers whose intimacy needs remain largely unfulfilled.

Furthermore, the capacity for intimacy determines the priest's conceptualization of God and readies him for the experience of God's presence and love in his life. He becomes aware of God's "affection" for him—the experience of which allows him to pass through loneliness into solitude. Aware of his fundamental rootedness in God's loving presence, he discovers a spontaneous ability to relate intimately both to himself and to those few friends and family members that constitute his core community of support. Without this ability for appropriate intimate relationships, the spiritual life of the priest is seriously handicapped and his psychological life will be restricted and unfulfilled. Not only does the priest's spiritual and emotional life suffer, his ministry and in particular his preaching will be sterile and only minimally effective.

The human condition makes intimacy a challenge in any age and culture. It appears to be a particularly vexing problem in our age. Technological breakthroughs as well as the materialistic and individualistic values of contemporary society have underscored the need for human connectedness and intimacy without facilitating their achievement.[13] Faced with the same difficulties confronting his brothers and sisters in society, the priest carries the added burden of the identity crisis discussed above. Without a healthy sense of identity, the achievement of authentic intimacy becomes heroic. The spiritual vitality of many priests today is a tribute to their heroic surrender to grace and their trust in a provident God who knows well their human needs and longings.

Integrity

The final preliminary issue to our discussion of the spirituality of the diocesan priest is that of integrity. While there is a good deal of denial here, priests, in moments of honesty, concede that it is possible for them to sell their souls in their service to the Church and to God's people. The vast majority of priests prize their loyalty to the gospel and to the Church whose mission it is to serve that gospel. They also strive to be obedient to the gospel and to the Church. Their loyalty and obedience to the Church, however, are not without complexity. They know it is not to be a blind and unthinking obedience and loyalty. Their challenge is to be true men of the Church and at the same time their own men. This fidelity to Church and conscience implies a certain tension in the life of the priest. The anxiety engendered by this tension is inevitable. Sooner or later, every priest struggling for personal integrity feels it. Because he believes the Church enjoys the abiding presence and guidance of the Holy Spirit, and because he trusts the integrity of Church leaders, there are relatively few issues of personal integrity that surface in his life. However, when they do surface, they indeed become issues of conscience. While he knows well the central role played by an informed and faithful conscience in the life of the Christian, the cognitive dissonance that follows upon what his own experience of priesthood and ministry tell him is in conflict with Church discipline or teaching is nonetheless painful. So painful, in fact, that some priests adapt an attitude of unthinking obedience and loyalty in order to escape the discomfort of being in tension with the Church they love. The consequent diminishment of personal integrity compromises the authenticity of their spiritual lives. They become, quite unwittingly, "kept men" who expect to be taken care of because of their supposed loyalty and fidelity to the institutional Church.

The antidote to this compromise in integrity is the courage to think. But thinking, the priest discovered in the seminary, can be dangerous. It may easily lead to uncertainty and uncertainty in turn evokes anxiety. To flee the existential anxiety of human life by embracing in a nonthinking and nonreflective manner the religious truths, traditions, and customs of his faith is to compromise his integrity. The priest, then, must not only read in the areas of theology, Scripture, and the human sciences, he must think about and reflect upon that which he has read. He must think about and reflect upon his lived experience as a human being, Christian, and priest. His faith is meant to be integrated into the fiber of his life, for failing to do so blocks his ability to minister as a mature person of integrity. He may preach the gospel, but his congregation senses that he has yet to live it.

The task of achieving and maintaining the priest's integrity is often compounded by his family of origin. If he comes from a dysfunctional family or enters the seminary and priesthood with serious authority issues, his personal integrity often appears to be under constant attack by the most reasonable expectations and directives of his superiors. The nature of the priest's relationship with his mother and father becomes a reliable indicator of the degree of difficulty he will encounter in his quest for personal integrity. Without a sense of personal integrity, the priest's spiritual life evolves into nothing more than sentimental exercises that serve to quiet the disturbing eruptions of his bad conscience. The guilt of his bad conscience often goes unrecognized for, in his own eyes, he is a good priest, clearly obedient to his Church. Where this is the case, the priest may suffer from clinical depression resulting from his repressed or denied guilt. The implications for his morale and spiritual life are evident.

Towards a Spirituality of the Diocesan Priest

Presbyteral spirituality, as all authentic Christian spiritualities, involves the disciplined self-surrender to the saving power of the paschal mystery. The context and environment of the priest's ministry and especially the distinctive character of his priestly ordination allow us to speak of a spirituality that is proper to the diocesan priest. Yet the specific character of presbyteral spirituality should not be exaggerated. Richard Schwartz observes that the spirituality of priests is essentially the spirituality of the Church. "Although shaped and formed by a distinctive role among the people of God, at its most basic level presbyteral spirituality is ecclesial. The priority given to the image of the people of God in *Lumen gentium* affirms the ecclesial spirituality common to all, making ministerial priests more like the people they serve than different from them."[14] With this caveat in mind, we turn now to the spirituality of the diocesan priest.

Before the Second Vatican Council, the diocesan priest's spirituality was grounded in what was understood to be his ontological status as a priest of the Church. This status conferred upon him powers that were held in awe by believers and at least respected by nonbelievers. His priestly identity was concomitant with his power to consecrate, forgive, anoint and bless. With these powers came the responsibility to lead a holy life befitting his presbyteral status. The celebration of Eucharist, praying the breviary, the rosary, and other devotions were the source and fuel of his spirituality. Serving the poor, visiting the sick, educating children, instructing converts, and preaching to his people also became mainstays of his spiritual life. While undeniably ministerial, his spirituality was focused on the ascetical and devotional aspects of the inner life. He said his prayers so that he might be a good priest and serve his God and people well.

A shift in emphasis has occurred since the council. The origins of the shift surely go back to the early decades of our century, which witnessed the beginnings of the modern liturgical movement, if not beyond. The shift is more developmental than disjunctive, for it builds on the traditional staples of priestly spirituality. It enjoys, nonetheless, a distinctive character that continues to evolve and emerge. In the past, the priest prayed in order to preach. Now, following the insight of Abraham Heschel, it may be claimed that the priest preaches in order to pray.[15] He understands the inherent mutuality and interdependence between his ministry and spiritual life. The decision to pray is arguably the most important decision the priest makes concerning his spiritual life. At the same time, the decision to exercise priestly ministry is equally central to his spirituality. The decisions to pray and to minister both serve the spirituality of the diocesan priest, for they are the form and structure of his life in grace. The emerging spirituality of the diocesan priest, therefore, may be thought of as a dialectical spirituality that is rooted in his life of faith and prayer and at the same time shaped and forged by the exercise of his ministerial priesthood. It is in the latter pole of the dialectic that we discover those characteristics that allow us to speak of a spirituality proper to the diocesan priest.

The function and scope of priestly ministry has been significantly reshaped over the past twenty-five years. Postconciliar research in the areas of ecclesiology, ministry, and priesthood have generated in turn issues and questions relating to the spirituality of priests. The conciliar document *Lumen gentium*, for example, reclaimed the traditional understanding of the Church as mystery and as the people of God.[16] In the Counter-Reformation era, the Church perceived itself as the center of God's saving plan for the salvation of the world. Now, in the conciliar era of Vatican II, emphasis is placed on the Church as servant to a graced and redeemed humanity. This retrieved understanding of Church focuses attention on the Church as a people-centered community rather than as a priest-centered one. The priest in turn is regarded as one who serves a people-centered community, a very different emphasis from that of the priest-centered Church.[17] In a people-centered Church, while the ministry of the priest continues to hold a central and unique place in the life of the community, it is exercised as one ministry among other ministries.[18] In a Church understood as the people of God, the priest functions as servant of God's people and as one whose ministry is exercised in cooperation with and interdependent upon other diverse ministries in the Church.[19] Since Vatican II, the priest's ministry is less solitary and more communal and as much diaconal as sacral.[20]

In a recent article on the priesthood, Michael Himes reflects on the diaconal and episcopal dimensions of ministry:

> Catholics have long been accustomed to speak of a universal priesthood in the church, a priesthood of all the faithful. I am suggesting that, as there is a universal presbyterate, so too there are a universal episcopate and a universal diaconate in the church, an episcopate and diaconate of all the faithful. All are called to the episcopal function of maintaining the unity of the community. All are called to the presbyteral function of responsibility to and for the word. All are called to the diaconal function of direct service to those within and outside the community. The vocation to these universal ministries is given in baptism, which is the principal sacrament of ministry.[21]

Himes' insights into the universal episcopate and diaconate have significance for both the morale and spirituality of the diocesan priest. There is no question that the diocesan priest is called to be a servant of God's people and to work to further justice and peace. Also, it is clear that the priest participates in the episcopal ministry of furthering the unity and mission of the Church. His primary ministry, however, remains his sacral service "to and for the word." Whenever the priest overidentifies with either the diaconal or episcopal ministries, he risks both the loss of focus in his ministry and his identity as priest. Furthermore, his morale is lowered when he is expected by others or himself to be equally invested in the diaconal and episcopal ministries while being fully committed to his ministry as priest.

These significant developments in our understanding of Church and the ministry have elicited a new style of presbyteral ministry. No longer the final word on all parish matters, the diocesan priest, as servant-leader, is a facilitator and enabler of numerous and varied ministries within his parish. Though captain of the team, he is not to forget that he remains a member of the team. Instead of issuing directives and orders, the priest is called to a collaborative style of pastoral ministry. There is a certain asceticism in collaborative ministry, in identifying and fostering the ministerial gifts of others, in listening to the concerns of parishioners, in trusting their experiences and vision. Few diocesan priests would deny this. Nor would they deny the *kenosis*, the call to humility and self-gift that is at the heart of servant ministry.[22]

A Spirituality of the Word

A priest is a man to whom the word has been entrusted. He is, before all else, the minister and servant of the word of God.[23] Karl Rahner writes: "This efficacious word has been entrusted to the priest. To him has been given *the* word of God. That makes him a priest. For that reason it can be said it is he to whom has been entrusted the word."[24] *Presbyterorum ordinis* states that "priests . . . have as their primary duty the proclamation of the gospel of God to all."[25] Unless grounded in authentic holiness of life and maturity of personality, this most serious obligation and responsibility of the priest will remain substantially unfulfilled. And so he prays that he might preach. But as Heschel has observed, he also preaches that he might pray. Perhaps the dialectical dimension to the priest's spirituality is most clearly manifested in

his ministry of preaching. For not only has the council reminded him of his primordial obligation to preach the gospel,
it has at the same time encouraged him to preach at weekday
celebrations of Eucharist as well as at the Sunday liturgy.[26]
Each day he is encouraged to offer a homily, each day he is
shaped and formed by the word of God that he proclaims.
This call to daily preaching, I believe, is at the heart of the
diocesan priest's spirituality. It requires, day after day, the
reading of the Lectionary, prayer and reflection on the readings of the day, and the crafting of the homily itself. Taken
seriously, this responsibility to preach God's word becomes
the ground and foundation of the diocesan priest's spirituality.
Conversely, the call to preach the gospel at Sunday and daily
liturgies becomes an intolerable burden to the spiritually shal-
low. In Rahner's words, "the word of God in the mouth of
a priest empty of faith or love is a judgment more terrible
than all versification and all poetic chatter in the mouth of
a poet who is not really one. It is already a lie and a judgment upon a man, if he speaks what is not in him; how much
more, if he speaks of God while he is godless."[27] To the priest
faithful to prayer and reflection, to quietly listening to the voice
of God as revealed to him in the events of the day, the call
to preach becomes the anchor of his spirituality.

The dialectical dimension is likewise found in the other
manifestations of ministry that fill the day-to-day life of the
diocesan priest. In his teaching he is taught—not only by the
experience of grace and truth he finds in his students but also
by the power of the word of liberation, forgiveness, and healing
that he shares with his listeners. In his counseling he is counseled. Reminding the counselee of God's understanding and
acceptance, he discovers that he, too, is accepted and understood in spite of his own brokenness and human limitations.
The graced connectedness that is regularly experienced in the
process of pastoral counseling refines the priest's spirit and
sustains him when confronted by his own doubts and anxie-
ties. The courage that he witnesses in the lives of his parishion-

ers encourages his own soul to face bravely the responsibilities of Christian discipleship. In visiting the sick, the patient in himself is uplifted. In consoling the grieving, he finds consolation. In his ministry of leadership he finds guidance and direction from those in his congregation blessed with the charism of leadership. In serving the needs of the poor, his own poverty of soul finds relief. While Christian ministry is dialectical in the sense just described, the priest's service to the word of God remains the cornerstone and linchpin of his spirituality. It is especially in his Eucharistic presiding and preaching that his spirit is transformed by the saving grace of Jesus Christ crucified and risen. At the Lord's table, breaking word and bread, blessing cup and covenant, the mark of his priesthood emerges in bold relief.

The spirituality of the diocesan priest, therefore, is a spirituality of proclamation. Through years of faith and formation he has come to personally know the power of the proclaimed word.[28] Through years of being submerged in the human condition he has encountered the power of grace unfolding in the depths of his own life and the lives of his people. His preaching, he discovers, is aptly thought of as the art of naming grace.[29] The art of preaching, the art of naming grace, brings the priest into realms of mystery and meaning. His challenge, he discovers, is to acquire that subtlety of soul and flexibility of intelligence demanded of his craft. Without these qualities, his preaching will be pedantic and lifeless. He may well invoke the name of God while failing to name the experience of God in the lives of his listeners. He may speak of mystery and of that which really matters, but he will speak as one not personally touched by the mystery of grace nor inspired by his soul's thirst for meaning. But let him take seriously the call to preach and he will discover that refinement and passion of spirit common to the poet and mystic.[30]

Before proceeding to the final section of this chapter, I want to remind the reader that the emphasis I have placed on preaching in the context of Eucharist as the linchpin of the diocesan priest's spirituality is not meant to diminish the more traditional mainstays of his spirituality: The Liturgy of the Hours, the celebration of penance, days of retreat and recollection, spiritual reading and direction, Marian devotion—all these sustain the priest in his quest for holiness and, of course, give authority and power to his preaching and ministry.

Prayer and Grace

It has already been noted that the decision to pray is the most critical decision an individual makes in relation to his or her spiritual life. The psalms and lessons of the Church, whether scriptural or patristic, remain an important source of spiritual nourishment for priests and Christians in general. There is a growing awareness, however, that some form of contemplative prayer is vital to the life of the priest. When priests speak of their spiritual lives, more often than not they speak of a sacred time during the day when they enter into a period of solitude and wordless prayer. This quiet time of waiting on the Lord, of faithful listening to God's spirit, becomes central to their life in the Spirit. It is in silent prayer that the priest, in listening to the depths of his spirit, is able to discover what is going on in his own soul. In these periods of silent prayer he finds the grace to name what it is that he is experiencing at this particular point in his journey. In turn, this spiritual self-knowledge allows him to listen to God from his heart. Not only does he find the direction God wishes him to take personally but he finds himself able to discern what it is that God is asking of him in his ministry as priest. Finding time for contemplative prayer remains a significant challenge for the diocesan priest. The almost unbearable demands upon his time make this challenge all the more difficult. The call to contemplative prayer remains, nonetheless, as imperative for the diocesan priest as it is for the priest in religious life.

Recalling the final words of Bernanos' *Diary of a Country Priest*, the diocesan priest knows that "all is grace." His commitment to prayer and ministry brings him into daily contact with the hidden workings of grace. In his preaching, the diocesan priest proclaims the word of God and in doing so names the grace of everyday living. In terms of his own life, he comes to see that both the pain and the privilege of the priesthood are rooted in grace. The inescapable loneliness of celibacy is graced. So, too, the fraternity of the priesthood is graced. When his preaching stirs hearts and deepens faith, there is grace. When his ministry is ineffective and his words ring empty, there, too, is grace. When his motives are misjudged and his limitations laid bare, it is grace that sustains him. It is grace that sustains everything, and all about is the hidden presence of the Spirit. The priest comes to believe, sooner or later, that grace is "loose in the world."[31] No force is able ultimately to restrain this loving grace loosed upon the world: not the sinfulness of the world, not the sinfulness of the Church, not his own sinfulness. Herein is the source of his hope and courage.

Joseph Campbell speaks of the hero as an individual who "has given his or her life to something bigger than oneself."[32] Indeed, the priest has given his life to something bigger than himself—the gospel of Christ and the building of the reign of God in history. He preaches the word in season and out, when it is joyfully received and when it is cynically rejected. While in need of ministry himself, he ministers to others, while wounded himself, he heals and gives comfort. Though broken in heart and spirit, he reconciles and forgives, though anxious himself, he gives courage and hope to the alienated and estranged. In the name of God and the Christ and the Spirit, he has set out on a journey fraught with dangers and dragons. His quest is to set people free with the freedom and grace of the gospel and in doing so to renew the face of the earth. The grail after which he seeks is the treasure hidden within the hearts of all men and women: to find their true selves in God, for therein lies their salvation. As the diocesan priest continues to discover his true identity as a member of the people of God with a unique and heroic mission to fulfill, he will discover the spirituality that is properly his own.

Conclusion

The spirituality of the diocesan priest emerges from his ministry as priest and preacher. He prays in order to preach and preaches in order to pray. He prays in order to serve and serves in order to pray. Whatever he does is grounded in the gift of grace, and in the very doing of what priests do, his soul is renewed. It is possible, therefore, to speak of the spirituality of the priest as a "dialectical spirituality." The dialectical nature of the diocesan priest's spirituality is most clearly seen in his preaching, in his service to the word of God. The encouragement to preach a homily at daily celebrations of Eucharist as well as Sunday celebrations is the major structural development in the spirituality of the priest emanating from the Second Vatican Council. For the daily homily demands prayer and reflection, study and contemplation. It calls the priest to acquire the imagination of the novelist and the heart of the poet. The creative act of preaching, in which the word of God transforms preacher and hearer and names the grace of everyday life, serves as the linchpin of the diocesan priest's spiritual life. To preach well and effectively, to be servant-leader to the Catholic community, to evangelize society, is, indeed, a heroic mission—the mission of the priest.

Have we reached a point where it is possible to name the spirituality of the diocesan priest? I am not sure. Robert Schwartz speaks of the spirituality of priests as an ecclesial spirituality.[33] Certainly, he is correct. However, this description can equally be attributed to other spiritualities. The same can be said of "dialectical spirituality." While "presbyteral spirituality" sounds somewhat pretentious, it is perhaps the simplest and most appropriate term for the evolving spirituality of the diocesan priest. Named or unnamed, we are witnessing the emergence of a spirituality that is uniquely appropriate to the diocesan priest.

Notes

1. Thomas O'Meara, "The Ministry of the Priesthood and Its Relationship to the Wider Ministry in the Church," *Seminaries in Dialogue* 11 (September 1985) 6.

2. Gerald May states that "spirituality consists of an experienced and interpreted relationship among human beings and the mystery of creation." *Will and Spirit* (San Francisco: Harper & Row, 1982) 22.

3. *Spiritual Renewal of the American Priesthood* (United States Catholic Conference, 1973) 3.

4. *Reflections on the Morale of Priests* (United States Catholic Conference, 1988) 7-8.

5. Thomas O'Meara, *Theology of Ministry* (New York: Paulist, 1983) especially chapters 1 and 6.

6. O'Meara, "The Ministry of the Priesthood and Its Relationship to the Wider Ministry in the Church," 3.

7. Andrew M. Greeley, *American Catholics Since the Council: An Unauthorized Report* (Chicago: The Thomas More Press, 1985) 115.

8. Ibid., 114-115.

9. Ibid., 112. Also see James Kelly and Tracy Schier, "Data and Mystery: A Decade of Studies on Catholic Leadership," *America* (November 18, 1989) 345-350.

10. Philip Rieff, *The Triumph of the Therapeutic* (New York: Harper Torchbooks, 1968).

11. See Joann Wolski Conn's *Spirituality and Personal Maturity* (New York: Paulist, 1989). Conn notes that "in the biblical vision, spiritual maturity is deep and inclusive love. It is the loving relationship to God and others born of the struggle to discern where and how God is present in the community, in ministry, in suffering, in religious and political dissension, and in one's own sinfulness. . . . Maturity is understood primarily as a matter of relationship" (p. 16).

12. *The Catholic Priest in the United States, Psychological Investigations* (United States Catholic Conference, 1972) 16.

13. See John Naisbitt's *Megatrends* (New York: Warner Books, 1982).

14. Richard Schwartz, *Servant Leaders of the People of God* (New York: Paulist, 1989) 54. Schwartz continues: "Formed by the same word, nourished by the same eucharist, called to the same quest for holiness and justice, priests and people are able to serve one another" (p. 54).

15. Abraham Joshua Heschel, *Quest for God: Studies in Prayer and Symbolism* (New York: Crossroad, 1982). Heschel writes, "Preach in order to pray. Preach in order to inspire others to pray. The test of a true sermon is that it can be converted to prayer" (p. 80).

16. *Lumen gentium*, ch. 2. Also see *Gaudium et spes,* especially the preface. In *Vatican Council II: The Conciliar and Post-Conciliar Documents,* ed. Austin Flannery (Northport, N.Y.: Costello, 1975).

17. I am indebted to Richard Schwartz's treatment of this development in *Servant Leaders of the People of God,* 5-6.

18. See Thomas O'Meara's "Ministry of the Priesthood and Its Relationship to the Wider Ministry in the Church," 2, as well as his important book, *Theology of Ministry.*

19. See *The Continuing Education of Priests: Growing in Wisdom, Age, and Grace* (United States Catholic Conference, 1985).

20. O'Meara, "The Ministry of the Priesthood and Its Relationship to the Wider Ministry in the Church."

21. Michael J. Himes, "Making Priesthood Possible: Who Does What and Why," *Church* (Fall 1989) 7.

22. See *As One Who Serves: Reflections on the Pastoral Ministry of Priests in the United States* (United States Catholic Conference, 1977).

23. Karl Rahner, "Priest and Poet," *Theological Investigations*, vol. 3, trans. Karl-H. and Boniface Kruger (New York: Helicon, 1967) 303.

24. Ibid., 307.

25. *Presbyterorum ordinis,* in Walter Abbott, *The Documents of Vatican II* (Guild Press, 1966) 538-539.

26. *Sacrosanctum concilium,* in Walter Abbott, *The Documents of Vatican II,* ch. 2, no. 52, p. 155. "The homily . . . is to be highly esteemed as a part of the liturgy itself. . . ."

27. Rahner, "Priest and Poet," 308.

28. "The word of God in the mouth of the priest wants therefore, if it is to be spoken rightly, to absorb and subject to itself the life of the priestly individual. It wants to be made manifest in him. But then it calls upon the whole man and lays claim to him with everything that is his." Ibid., 313.

29. See Mary Catherine Hilkert's "Naming Grace: A Theology of Proclamation," *Worship* 60 (September 1986) 434-449.

30. See Rahner, Priest and Poet," 294-317.

31. See Thomas O'Meara's *Loose in the World* (New York: Paulist, 1974).

32. Joseph Campbell, *The Power of Myth* (New York: Doubleday, 1988) 123. See especially ch. 5, "The Hero's Adventure."

33. The subtitle of Robert Schwartz's *Servant Leaders of the People of God* is "An Ecclesial Spirituality for American Priests."

Priesthood Within the Context of Religious Life

Paul J. Philibert, O.P.

Christian religious are symbolic persons. Their lives are bound up with divine mysteries. Whether their symbolic existence is structured by monastic enclosure and a promise of stability or by apostolic mission and frequent itinerancy, all religious participate in some important common symbolic traits. First, their lives are focused upon the following of Christ along patterns devised and established by their religious founders. Some religious institutes concentrate upon a particular aspect of the mystery of Christ, for example, upon his cross, his precious blood, his sacred heart, or the mystery of the Eucharist. Others shape their following of Christ according to broad religious goals, as monastics do in building contemplative communities or as mendicants do in their mixed life of common prayer ordained to apostolic work. Nevertheless, all religious in varying degrees bind their lives into a symbolic pattern that is intended to realize with special intensity the visible effect of Christ's grace upon human society. Their own particular realization of Christian community is a prophetic statement about Christ's leavening presence in the world.

Religious are also symbolic persons in the solidarity they represent with brothers and sisters of the same religious family. We speak of their being partakers of a common charism.

This means that they agree in imitating the spirit and ideals of their founder and of other notable examples of successful living within their tradition. Moreover, they have a common sense of the esprit de corps and style of their community—a sense that derives as much from subtle, intuited customs as from constitutions and formal directories. Further, their charism governs the equilibrium or balance between intracommunity life and apostolic mission—with respect to both the frequency and the kind of ministry that pertains to the institute's charism. The symbolic character of religious is closely bound to the demands of the charism of their institute upon their manner of living and working.

The life of religious is also bound up with the Church. Religious are radically committed persons. (We used to say "consecrated" persons.) By making public vows or promises accepted by the Church, they foreclose one of the most tantalizing avenues of restlessness in life by choosing to remain perpetually a member of their institute and in that way a follower of Christ. This marks their lives with a symbolic quality of availability that is precious to the life of the Church. We count on religious to be true to their vows, and we look to them to model behavior that is a witness to a Christlike vision. We trust that their lives will manifest something important about what "Church" ought to look like in a given time and place.

In summary, whatever other dimensions may particularize their qualities of personality or activity, all religious have in common these fundamental symbolic relations to Christ, to their religious family, and to the Church. In addition, some male religious are called by their institutes, in pursuit of apostolic or pastoral aims coherent with each group, to assume Church office as ordained presbyters. The role of presbyter or priest is itself loaded with strong symbolic meaning, connecting the priest with Christ as a mediator of his hieratic actions within the Christian community. (David Power shows in his chapter how important is the symbolic construction of this role as presbyter—an analysis that has deep implications for the symbolic weight one gives to the role.)

In the following pages, I want to explore the interplay of these two symbolic continents: on the one hand, religious life as a personal identity and, on the other hand, priesthood as a role or office in the Church. As other essays in this volume indicate, there are many forces at play that have begun to reshape the Church's understanding of priesthood. Because of the particular continent of symbolic relations that religious inhabit, they will be especially sensitive to the shifting valences or meanings of the office of presbyter. A question much on the mind of both bishops and religious is whether priests who are religious will be able to supply for dwindling numbers of diocesan clergy so as to serve parishes threatened with the absence of a priest. This question, however, is closely related to the parallel questions of the identity of the clerical religious priest and the relations of his priesthood to his religious identity. In pursuit of clarifying those issues, I will proceed to make three arguments.

First, the symbolic relations of both religious and priests are concretely perceived within a present Church order that is marked by symbolic dislocation (a term I shall explain in my exposition). Second, all baptized Christians participate in varying ways in the one priesthood of Jesus Christ. From where does the identity of a religious who is also a priest derive? Third, what are some of the special contributions of priests from clerical religious institutes in the Church today?

Symbolic Dislocation

Symbols connect. We have seen some of the ways that the symbolic identity of religious connects them to Christ, to their institute, and to the Church. If these symbolic relations were uncomplicated or if they were not sometimes (as they are) in conflict with other relations, then it would be quite easy to understand the signification of the ecclesial identity of religious and quite simple to resolve passing difficulties. But, as observed before, religious institutes differ widely in spirit and purpose, some being distinct because of the explicit intention of their founder, others because of historical or cultural circumstances that have intervened.

In addition, the past century has introduced major adjustments in the ways in which most people understand the Church. Whatever categories one might choose to describe the phenomenon, it is fair to say that the prevailing ecclesiology of the post–Vatican II Church is quite different from the ecclesiology of either Vatican I or Trent. Some modern religious institutes were established precisely to embody the goals of a Counter-Reformation Church. Like these institutes, all religious are to some degree challenged to relocate their symbolic relation to the Church following a generation of theological effervescence.

There is a phenomenon, which I will call symbolic dislocation, that takes place when the connection between symbolically germane realities shifts in significant ways. For example, many religious in the early decades of this century or throughout the past few centuries would have understood that their symbolic relation to the Church warranted an unquestioning, blind obedience to the wishes of the Holy See. (The rules of some institutes effectively institutionalized such an interpretation of obedience.) But in the light of theological evolution since Vatican II, few institutes would any longer interpret their obedience to the Holy See so simplistically. Most would apply to a claim or demand of the Holy See a hermeneutic that would lead them through a consideration of the gospel in the light of their institute's charism, a consideration of their rule or constitution, and a communal discernment that would profit from the experience of their members. This might serve as an example of symbolic dislocation. The symbolic connection is maintained even while its aspects or interpretations shift in significant ways. In what follows, I would like to trace several examples of symbolic dislocation that influence the meaning of religious life and priesthood in today's Church.

1. *The Constantinian Church.* The biblical, catechetical, and liturgical renewals that paved the way for the Second Vatican Council rendered the Church more sensitive to the primacy of the New Testament Word of God as the source and norm of Christian faith. In addition, both archaeological and philological research—especially traditions research—have given us a much more concrete appreciation for the figure of Jesus and for the formation of the apostolic Church than was available to medieval and baroque theologians, who created the classical syntheses that became the seminary manuals of the eighteenth and nineteenth centuries. As the drafts of the documents of Vatican II began to appear in the early 1960s, manifesting in important ways the integration of recent scholarship, some theologians raised the issue of symbolic dislocation by pointing out the inconsistency between the simple, prophetic origins of the Jesus movement on the one hand, and the triumphalistic, hierarchical organization of the present-day Vatican bureaucracy on the other.

"Triumphalism" was much discussed in the 1960s. One theologian framed the question by suggesting that the time had come to disenfranchise the "Constantinian Church." His argument ran as follows: Once the persecuted Jesus movement emerged from hiding with the crowning of the first Christian Emperor, Constantine, it became transformed into an established Church. Constantinian Christianity dethroned Roman religion and replaced it with a parallel apparatus. In this way, Christianity lost its original spontaneity and cultural suppleness even as it gained security and status as an institution of Western culture. Christianity shaped the West, but it did so not just as a religious movement arising from the preaching and saving works of Jesus but rather as a religious movement that became embedded in distinct, culturally particular institutions it appropriated from the Roman world.

As political institutions in the West came and went, they were mirrored in the ecclesiastical structures of the Roman Church. The myth of the Holy Roman Empire, making the Christian princes of the West vassals of the pope, lasted almost a thousand years. This institutional arrangement provided stability and protection for the Roman Church, but at the cost of losing the initial flexibility and evangelism that marked the apostolic era.[1] Today, as the Church awakens to fresher images of its New Testament origins and as it becomes aware of its decidedly minority status among the peoples and religions of the earth, it becomes more evident that a Roman Church still structured along the lines of a triumphalistic, imperial bureaucracy is a symbolic dislocation of the Church's primordial meaning.

Of course, Christians believe that history emerges under the ruling providence of God. Therefore, the long evolution of papal power through two millennia has been guided by God's grace and mercy. But belief in God's providence and ultimate rule over history does not preclude the intrusion of finite human interests, which can impede or distort the success of God's plan for the world. The challenge before us, it seems to me, is not so much to judge the past as to respond to the present. And at present the perceptible need is more for an evangelical suppleness and leavening enculturation than for a centralized, international Roman bureaucracy.

The symbolic relations of both religious and priests to the Church universal will bear different symbolic weight depending upon which construction one gives to the Church's nature—that of a prophetic evangelical movement that transcends cultural limits or that of an imperial, hierarchical bureaucracy that exercises its spiritual governance in structures that are modeled upon (past) historical political institutions. In my view, the current symbolic dislocation is due to an unnecessary centralization and bureaucratization of Vatican government, which impedes the universal bishop and his curia from giving witness to the primordial poverty and simplicity of the Jesus movement. It follows that many issues of discipline within the Church would be framed differently if the Church's self-image were restructured to resemble more closely contemporary scholarship on Christian origins.

2. *The role of religious charism and priesthood.* From what was said in my introductory remarks, it is clear that a case could be made that the ministry of the priest-religious is shaped and bounded by the charism of his institute. The charism governs the expression of priestly office; the call to the institute and participation in its charism is somehow primary. If that were verifiable, then the symbolic relation of the priest-religious to the Church would be governed by the primacy of that institute's charism. In fact, things are frequently experienced differently.

With the possible exception of enclosed monastics, clerical religious institutes generally receive candidates who feel themselves called to priestly service in the Church. Commonly, candidates choose to enter a particular institute because they have been served pastorally by its members or because they have been impressed by and attracted to the preaching or pastoral guidance of an individual religious.

Among us Dominicans a great proportion of our members came to know the order and to join our ranks because of the parochial services that we rendered in various places. These days, campus ministry chaplaincies are the most likely seedbeds for vocations to the order. Both parish work and campus ministry are valid expressions of the Dominican charism. But here in the United States our involvement in concrete parochial service has become so dominant that some of our provinces realize only slightly or deficiently aspects of our charism that are more important historically and ideally. We have very few research scholars and very few itinerant preachers, proportionate to our numbers.

We share this symbolic dislocation of our relation to our own charism with other institutes. Generally, "religious communities of men came to this country in order to carry on their particular missions as those had been described in the European context, i.e., missions, seminaries, education, youth, etc. However, as the church rapidly grew, the religious found themselves more and more involved in parishes."[2] *Perfectae caritatis*, Vatican II's decree on religious life, called us to return to the original inspiration and spirit of our founder and thus to recapture our core charism. But we have found it difficult to do so for various reasons.

Our prototypical ministries are demanding and difficult. Our engagement with parishes is an institutional commitment difficult to put aside, both for financial reasons and for attachment reasons. Also, we do not easily attract candidates who are well suited to some of the more taxing expressions of the order's charism.

To the degree that an institute fails to achieve a realistic expression of its authentic charism, it suffers a symbolic dislocation that obscures its ecclesial role. The question of the relation of an individual who is both religious and priest to these two aspects of his ecclesial identity becomes more difficult as a result.

3. *Cultural conditions for ordination.* There are many dimensions of Church life that might be vulnerable to a hermeneutic of symbolic dislocation. But one more is of particular interest here, even though its analysis is especially sensitive and its resolution far from clear. That is the question of the cultural conditions for ordination in the Roman Church, namely, maleness, celibacy, and lifelong engagement.

Twenty-five years ago, celibacy was the more debated element in this set of conditions for ordination. Already then it was clear that a significant pool of candidates would be available for priestly service in the Church if married persons were accepted for ordination. Today maleness as a condition is the more vividly discussed.

The requirement that only males may be ordained is moot in large part because of the recent practice of the Episcopalians, the Christian body apparently closest to us in theology and

Church practice. They have admitted women to ordination as priest and bishop. It is not clear that there is a large number of Catholic women who do indeed desire priestly ordination or, put another way, that if ordained their numbers would significantly alleviate the present and foreseen shortage of diocesan clergy in the coming decades.[3] But that is not the most telling issue here. The key question, I think, is about the relation of presbyter to community or local Church.

What we see occurring in the North American Church is a strange transformation of Church polity whereby the Church's leaders are choosing to modify the most ancient and central characteristic of the local Church, namely, the celebration of the Lord's Day with the Eucharistic sacrifice, in order to maintain a much more peripheral discipline of Church order, namely, the conditions of maleness and celibacy for priestly ordination. The result is not only a denial of Eucharist to many local communities but also a transformation of Eucharistic piety from a sacramental to a devotional model.

The symbolic dislocation that is being made manifest in this case is a shift from an image of Eucharistic banquet as an act of the local Church animated by the Holy Spirit under the liturgical presidency of one of its members to an image of Eucharist as an act of a sacral figure, the presbyter, who serves the local community in a hieratic action that is relatively independent of time and place.[4] To the degree that the hieratic presbyteral image of Eucharist prevails, to that same degree the urgency to supply priests who fulfill the standing conditions for a hieratic persona (maleness, celibacy, lifelong commitment) will be salient. This touches the question of priests from religious communities in that the resolution of this issue will have some impact on their relationship to the local bishop.

Without a change of Church policy in these matters, the urgency to supply sacramental ministers for parishes will remain the dominating concern of bishops. Further, the popular expectations of priestly service may mitigate against some forms of ministry done by religious priests, such as presence to the marginated, direct service to the poor and oppressed, and even itinerant evangelization.

Consequently, the entire issue of symbolic dislocation brings to light that the interpretation that one gives to Church, to charism, and to requisite conditions for ordination will greatly modify the approach one will take to the relation between religious identity and priesthood. However, before trying to summarize the outcome of that issue, I want first to establish some important perspectives on the theology of priesthood.

Priesthood: Universal and Ministerial

All baptized Christians participate in varying ways in the one priesthood of Jesus Christ. Ordained priests participate in that mystery in a fuller manner, because by ordination they become "companions and helpers . . . who . . . humbly dedicate themselves to the work of sanctification. . . . Thus in performing sacred functions they can act as the ministers of Him who in the liturgy continually exercises His priestly office on our behalf by the action of His Spirit."[5] These sacred functions are, above all, the administration of the sacraments of the Church.

The laity, too, are associated with the life and mission of Christ and share in his priestly function of offering "spiritual worship for the glory of God and the salvation of [others]." They do this through the integrity and faith that they bring to their "ordinary married and family life, their daily labor, their mental and physical relaxation, if carried out in the Spirit, and . . . the hardships of life."[6] Clearly, then, both ordained and nonordained Christians participate in the mystery of Christ's priesthood, according to the teaching of Vatican II.

It is striking, however, that in the New Testament "no individual Christian is ever specifically identified as a priest."[7] Jesus receives many different titles in the Gospels—Messiah, Son of Man, Prophet, Son of God—but it is not until the late Epistle to the Hebrews (written probably after the destruction of the Temple in Jerusalem) that the title "High Priest" becomes a focal title for Jesus. These facts are very challenging to our popular piety.

It would be wrong, though, to judge that Jesus lacked an awareness of or a commitment to the function of an authentic priest. As Christian Duquoc points out, Jesus enters with freedom into the mystery of his own sacrificial death; he identifies his passover transformation as a "new temple" that replaces the old one (see Mark 14:58; John 2:19; 7:37ff). Further, the Old Testament priest did not function exclusively in offering sacrifice; he was as well a proclaimer of God's word and a teacher of the Law. Clearly Jesus fulfilled all these priestly functions.[8]

At the same time, as his words and deeds are recorded in the Gospels, Jesus refused to claim the title of priest for himself. That is not so surprising, since his mission was to call people beyond the ritual, cultic system of Judaism to a new law and a new commandment. His mission was to lead God's people beyond a closed covenant of law and prescribed ritual sacrifices into a new covenant where those who worship God worship not in the Temple but "worship in spirit and in truth" (John 4:24).

The Church's gradual elaboration of a theology of Christ as high priest arose from its identification of Christ's crucifixion as the perfect, transforming sacrifice that overcame the alienation between God and the chosen people. By the offering of this one perfect sacrifice, Christ has restored the covenant. Further, the mediation of Christ as priest is exercised henceforth in the heavenly sanctuary. In Hebrews (7:23-25) we read: "Further, the former priests were many in number, because death put an end to each one of them; but this one, because he remains for ever, has a perpetual priesthood. It follows, then, that the power to save those who come to God through him is absolute, since he lives for ever to intercede for them." In this vision of Hebrews, the priest is taken from among humans to intercede for them before God. He belongs to the human world and to the divine world in equal measure. In the human world, he intervenes on behalf of his brothers and sisters with God and communicates in human form the message of God to them. In the divine world, he is the vehicle to transmit God's life to us humans in human form.

Only Christ can fulfill these dynamics. In his person and in his holiness, he has full claim to divinity. In his solidarity with us by his participation in all that is human (apart from sin—Heb 4:15), Christ, the servant of God, is at one with us. Therefore, even in Hebrews, Christ's priesthood is not conceived according to a dynamic of solemn privilege, otherness, and inaccessible consecration but rather according to a dynamic of humble service as the God-man who emptied himself (Phil 2:6-8) even to the point of obedience unto death.[9]

But the tension that is evident in this theology of the Epistle to the Hebrews is expressed in two different tendencies that coexist in the Church. To return to the idea of symbolic values, the theology of priesthood can be expressed, first, in a symbolic construction that mirrors the sacrificial priesthood of Christ in a way that stresses the priest as a hierarch, someone consecrated to be set apart from the general mass of people, whose life is marked not only by special burdens but also by special solemnity and even privilege. To this set of images belongs the emphasis, strong in Counter-Reformation theology, upon ordination to priesthood as a transformation of the priest into an ontologically distinct person, empowered with supernatural force to effect sacramental change through the use of sacred rites. Here there is also a bias toward gradations of rank as classifications of participation in the mystery of Christ. The view is well known and founded in extensive theological reflection covering many centuries of Christian faith. It parallels an institutional model of church with a strong centralizing and authoritarian structure.

Another symbolic construction of priesthood stresses the priest as servant, modeled upon Christ's *kenosis*—the self-giving that made it possible for the eternal Word to lay aside "being in the form of God" (Phil 2:6) so as to enter into solidarity with our human race. The efficacy of Christ's sacrifice, in this view, depends upon his at-one-ment with those for whom he suffered. As he is at one with us, so we are offered access to be likewise at one with Christ. The tone of this symbolic construction is that of humility, compassion, and openness.

Theologically, these two views complement each another. Each has its foundations in biblical readings of God's plan. That is one of the reasons why a theology of priesthood is so very difficult and why it is so little developed at the present time in the Church. In recent centuries, the dominant tendency of magisterial statements has been toward the first, the hierarchical reading of priesthood, rather than toward a dialectical reading that holds both symbolic constructions in dynamic tension.

From our perspective of an examination of priesthood in the context of religious life, it is possible to argue that priests from religious institutes most likely will have a bias toward the second, the servant model of priesthood. At least that is the case I will try to make here.

Vatican II's decree on religious life expresses a general description of the role of religious in saying:

> Whatever the diversity of their spiritual endowments, all who are called by God to practice the evangelical counsels and who do so faithfully, devote themselves in a special way to the Lord. They imitate Christ the virgin and poor man (cf. Matt 8:20; Luke 9:58), who, by an obedience which carried Him even to death on the cross (cf. Phil 2:8), redeemed humankind and made them holy. As a consequence, impelled by a love which

> the Holy Spirit has poured out into their hearts (cf. Rom 5:5),
> these Christians spend themselves ever increasingly for Christ,
> and for His body the Church (cf. Col 1:24).[10]

The general thrust of religious life is a following of Christ that
is structured along the demands of the evangelical counsels
of poverty, chastity, and obedience. These demands are accepted as norms, which religious take as the highest values
of their lives, committing themselves by vows to strive per-
manently to imitate the self-emptying of Christ for the sake
of solidarity and service in grace with the Lord. The sense
of this form of Christian living, therefore, is that individuals
have been touched by grace to interpret the meaning of their
lives as fundamentally available to the movement of God's
Spirit in the Church. As noted above, there is a great variety
of expressions of this common call to religious life. Thus, some
institutes will stress monastic withdrawal while others stress
apostolic readiness and sacrificial self-giving in works of humility and compassion. But all these institutes, at base, express the symbolism of service after the pattern of Christ the
suffering servant.

It must be noted that *Perfectae caritatis* itself indicates that
its teaching must be interpreted in the context of the Dogmatic Constitution on the Church (no. 1). That constitution
(no. 40) teaches that *everyone* in the Church is called to perfection "regardless of their situation." The Holy Spirit is sent
by Christ to us all to inspire us from within "to love God with
[our] whole heart and [our] whole soul, with all [our] mind
and all [our] strength and that [we] might love one another
as Christ loved [us]."[11] Followers of Christ are chosen not
by reason of their accomplishments but by reason of God's
purpose and grace. Therefore, God's power in believers is
not constrained by their moral actions but is free to be expressed independently of ecclesiastical status, religious vows,
or public role.

A key issue, however, is the general signification of religious life within the overall organization of the Church. *Per-*

fectae caritatis calls it "a blazing emblem of the heavenly kingdom" (no. 1), indicating that those who imitate Christ more nearly, through their vows, and follow Christ more freely make a sign of the power of the Holy Spirit in contemporary Christian life. In this way, religious life in general, whatever the concrete expression of different religious institutes, is a prophetic statement about God's power in this world. The decree on renewal of religious life states: "The more ardently [religious] unite themselves to Christ through a self-surrender involving their entire lives, the more vigorous becomes the life of the Church and the more abundantly her apostolate bears fruit."[12]

Concretely, the effects of this decree over the past twenty-five years have led American religious in large part away from fixed, institutional commitments and increasingly toward direct personal involvement with the victims of injustice, oppression, and poverty. This is not because the decree asked directly for such a change of social agency, but rather because indirectly these consequences flowed from the decree's insistence upon a rededication of religious to their founding charism: "It serves the best interests of the Church for communities to have their own special character and purpose. Therefore loyal recognition and safekeeping should be accorded to the spirit of founders, as also to all the particular goals and wholesome traditions which constitute the heritage of each community."[13] So we have found religious men and women in the last two decades becoming the animating forces behind new expressions of apostolic charity in the areas of work for justice and peace, the liberation of the oppressed, and direct compassionate service to the marginated. In some cases, religious have taken prophetic stances over against diocesan bureaucracies in the name of their newly rediscovered call to represent their charism in favor of the oppressed. In other cases, religious have moved away from service in schools and hospitals so as to express a greater mobility and accessibility to the most needy in our society.

Such changes have occasionally been the source of conflict and have disappointed those who have come to expect taken-for-granted services within ecclesiastical institutions. Yet the fundamental dynamic is clear. Religious are themselves somewhat marginated people, possessing special flexibility because of their obedience to the gospel and their institute's charism in the service not of one parish or one diocese but rather of the Church as a whole.[14]

To pause for a moment, then, in this argument, let me say that if there are two tendencies in the symbolization of Catholic priesthood, one symbolizing the priest as hierarch, the other as servant, then the more coherent tendency for religious who are priests is the latter. I mentioned earlier the issue of where priests who are religious derive their identity. I claim that on the basis of the teaching of Vatican II, the identity of the priest who is also a religious is derived more fundamentally from his religious charism than from his ordination. His priestly office is a role that is in the service of his fundamental religious identity, which is the following of Christ in the tradition and according to the charism of his own religious family. Note, however, that in drawing this conclusion, I am using a dominant servant model of priesthood and am abstracting somewhat from problems that frequently exist for religious priests who serve as pastors and assistant pastors in parishes.

Using an analogy with the life and ministry of Jesus, I would say that the priestly role of the religious priest is in the service of a life that is in its symbolic totality an epiphany of grace. Vatican II's Dogmatic Constitution on Divine Revelation describes the whole of Jesus' earthly existence as revelation: "Jesus perfected revelation by fulfilling it through His whole work of making Himself present and manifesting Himself: through His words and deeds, His signs and wonders, but especially through His death and glorious resurrection from the dead and final sending of the Spirit of truth."[15] For all priests, but especially in this context for religious priests, the priestly sacramentalizing role is a form of interaction with the Christian community, whose ritual power and social effectiveness draw upon the whole complex of actions and faith attitudes that constitute the "following of Christ." The religious who is a priest maintains practices of religious discipline and spirituality that have been inculcated precisely to form a quality of faith and a spirit of service identifiable as belonging to a particular religious family.

Most religious institutes treasure the formative influence and the moral support offered by living in community. The importance of this element of religious life varies from institute to institute. But in general, it is in the mutual exchanges and the shared praxis of common prayer and reciprocal fraternal service that religious are formed in the charism of their institute, are corrected and reformed throughout their lives, and are sent in mission to their apostolic works.

A final point in this section: Might it be easier and more appropriate for priests who are religious to be enablers of lay apostles than it is for diocesan pastors? There is no juridical or institutional reason for this to be the case. But given the examination of the way in which religious priests appropriate their presbyteral service, it may sometimes be easier for a religious to see his priesthood more as servant than as hierarch and to feel a fundamental sympathy for the nonordained who feel called to invest their lives substantially in the service of the Church. Religious share with such laity many threads of experience touching the web of religious meanings that bind them to a desire for a deeper closeness to Christ and a deeper self-giving in the service of Christ's body.

If such is sometimes the case, it is a blessing for a Church that is on the brink of what Pope John Paul II calls a new missionary frontier. In his apostolic exhortation on the mission of the laity, the Pope says that the new missionary frontier involves not going off to new continents, but rather a new effort of reevangelization that will employ "a mature and responsible lay faithful."[16] "The lay faithful participate, for their part, in the threefold mission of Christ as Priest, Prophet, and King.''[17] The focus of the Pope's exhortation is to call all the baptized into a work of ''restoration,'' which will reestablish creation in all its original value. The laity restore the world first of all through their secular work, done in faith with justice and integrity. In addition, there are places where their participation is needed in the administration of the rites of the Church, its catechesis, and its pastoral service.

In our own country, we have known already twenty-five years of ecclesial service by the nonordained, notably in the work of religious education. With the great diversification of ministries that is now occurring, laity have become engaged in a great variety of Church service. One of the chief responsibilities of priests in the decades just ahead will be to facilitate the smooth collaboration of such lay ministers in the apostolic works of the Church. Because of their primary identification with their institute's charism rather than with a hierarchical office, priests from religious institutes can make the contribution with particular grace of calling, initiating, and supporting the nonordained in the new ministries of our changing Church.

The Contribution of Religious to Priestly Ministry

There are, I think, some special contributions that religious make as priests because of their peculiar commitments. In no way do I mean to insinuate that priests from religious institutes make a pastorally superior contribution to the Church simply because of their religious status. There are many diocesan priests who are more effective, more talented, and more influential than priests who are religious. Rather, here I want to suggest some of the ways that priests from religious institutes can typically impact upon the life of the local Church.

Religious are meant to be witnesses to spiritual freedom by their life style. The vows of religious constitute a twofold moral dynamic that restructures their lives in a radical way. In the first dynamic, the vows signify an intense attachment to the reign of God preached by Jesus. Poverty, chastity, and obedience have apocalyptic overtones: I invest everything in this good news of Jesus and entrust everything to the promise of the reign of God. Only in the context of Jesus' preaching can the praxis of the vows look like anything but foolishness and masochism. But Jesus' preaching proclaims that the reign of God is slowly growing secretly in our midst, that God asks for a wild abandon to sell everything and come follow, and that God will provide more generously for those who trust in the reign of God than God has already done for the beauties of creation. Freedom here is learned in love through a discipline of unceasing effort to come to know Jesus the Christ and his promise ever more deeply.

In the second dynamic, the vows represent a voluntary detachment from aspects of life that can scatter and dissipate human energies. This renunciation is for the sake of a more intense engagement with a focal reality: first, with the person of Christ as friend and Savior and, second, with the needs of the body of the whole Christ—the Church. The renunciations made in the tradition of the vows of poverty, chastity, and obedience are not, however, simple, straightforward acts, made once for all. The vows have as their matter elements of human existence that are central to every life—owning, loving, and willing. All three of these elements have the capacity to shape our self-understanding. In fact, by approaching the fundamental realities of owning, loving, and willing in the manner of the evangelical counsels—"sell all you have and give it to the poor," "leave father and mother and family," "come, follow me"—religious do shape their self-understanding as being readily accessible to the will of God and available to God's Spirit.

Like all other persons, religious have the same capacity to make unrealistic romantic promises under the influence of self-inflating fantasies and then renege. Just as no couple on

their wedding day could possibly have an adequate understanding of what they are getting themselves into, so no religious at the moment of pronouncing vows has a full enough
appreciation of what God is asking for in the mystery of
his or her vocation. Yet in religious life, as in marriage, the
strongest aspect of witness comes not from the glorified moment in which one pronounces the vows but from the day-
by-day renewal of willingness to begin again the always powerful struggle against self-preoccupation and narcissism in the
service of God's call to a new form of life that is one's vocation.

Religious find the support for this continual reengagement
with their demanding vocation through growth in prayer. *Perfectae caritatis* calls this a need ''to develop a life hidden with
Christ in God'' and urges religious to ''cultivate the spirit
of prayer and the practice of it.''[18] Prayer lies at the heart
of the identity of religious. In many ways, both the joy and
the efficacy of the life of religious are tied up with the authenticity of their prayer. The mature prayer of those who have
spent years and decades growing in prayer is increasingly silent, simplified, and simplifying. God needs an acquiescent
spirit to transform all that is ordinary into a graced sign of
divine, loving presence.

The first contribution of religious clergy that I point out,
then, is spiritual freedom. But that means mostly enabling
God's freedom within themselves, becoming free enough from
compulsions and from illusions to enter the deepest core of
themselves without fear before God and to proceed into action from that central core. Each institute has such people.
Probably no institute has only people of that sort. Nonetheless, it pertains to the very meaning of religious life that the
vows have the power and means to call those so chosen into
a ''life with God.''

A second contribution of religious to priesthood is the special qualities that they bring to their exercise of public ministry. We can caricature these qualities or overdo or oversimplify
them, but we do recognize something like traditional traits

in most religious orders. We speak of Franciscan warmth, Benedictine hospitality, Jesuit cultivation and learning, Dominican doctrinal intensity, and so on. There is something real here. In many cases, religious seminarians receive a longer or more intense intellectual academic training for priesthood. In some cases, their seminary training incorporates in a significant way a study of the spirituality and literature of the religious order or congregation, and this adds a special flavor to the intellectual life of the group. In any case, religious can often challenge the local Church and its presbyterate to esteem values that are illuminated with special clarity by their fidelity to their religious family's charism.

In a particular way, it sometimes happens that the preaching and liturgical leadership of priests who are religious are notably more nourishing than the pastoral practice of diocesan parishes. This may be because religious priests can profit from the richer context of religious communities where the Liturgy of the Hours and other observances of the common life are carried out with regularity and sensitivity. When clerical religious do succeed in achieving equilibrium between their religious identity and their priestly role, this usually leads to greater vigor both in their pastoral service and in their communal exchanges. It is often the case that such houses of religious attract devout Christians from the local Church to share in their prayer and their hospitality. This dimension has been historically an important facet of religious life since the earliest days of the monastic movement.

By way of conclusion, it seems clear that since Vatican II American religious have repossessed important aspects of their charism, studying with renewed interest and enthusiasm the story and the mandate of their founders. It seems to me equally clear that there is still much that needs to be done to reclaim that mandate and repossess that charism.

Most religious institutes are about equally divided today between those who were trained in programs of religious formation before Vatican II and those who have known only the

postconciliar Church. The pre–Vatican II formation had many
elements that institutionalized characteristic forms of discipline
in prayer, renunciation, and service. Many older religious
feel that their institutes practically "apostacized" from the
traditions of their charism by letting go of the strong elements
of social control in the old formation programs. Postconciliar
formation programs at various times in the last three decades
have doubtlessly erred by way of naiveté in trusting too simply
the good will and presumed maturity of young persons eager
to enter and be identified with the institute but lacking much
insight or experience, either with regard to the institute's age-
old traditions or with regard to their own moral capacities.

In the face of the undeniable chaos that coexists in most
religious families along with much that is good and apostol-
ically effective, clerical religious institutes have a particular
challenge. Unless they firmly own and articulately define their
own relation to their institute's charism in such a way as to
relate it positively to the needs of the contemporary American Church, they will find it both increasingly difficult to avoid
being co-opted into more diocesan parochial service and also
difficult to elicit from their own members a quality of community life that is worthy of their own religious tradition.

There are many examples of what I have called symbolic
dislocation among priests from religious institutes whose lives
have become patterned on the life-style of parish clergy because of their assignment to parochial ministry. There are
similar examples of religious priests who have become so invested in the work of a particular career—university teaching, research, social-action ministry—that their life lacks the
depth and balance that I have tried to describe as typical traits
of priests who are members of religious institutes.

There will always be valid exceptions to rules about life-
styles. What we should attend to, however, is the special potential of this moment of reespousal to the renewal of religious
life called for by Vatican II. It aims at a symbolic integrity

that can offer the Church a unique and important witness to the function that religious can play.

We can be bridges across a number of discontinuities— priestly role versus interior life, hierarchical office versus collaborative ministry, apostolic engagement versus fraternal commitment. If we are to do this, we will need to be more attentive to the subtle complexities of the demands made by our identities as religious and our roles as ordained clergy. Success in so doing can only benefit everyone involved.

Notes

1. M.-D. Chenu, *La Parole de Dieu, II: L'Evangile dans le temps,* "La Fin de l'Ere Constantinienne" (Paris: Les Editions du Cerf, 1964) 17–36.

2. John Grindel, C.M., unpublished manuscript. When Fr. (later Bishop) Edward Fenwick, O.P., founded the Dominicans in the United States, his intent was to establish the order near Baltimore with a college and university. Because of the pastoral needs of the growing American Church, Archbishop Carroll asked Father Fenwick to go to Kentucky, where he founded Saint Rose Parish and Priory near Springfield. While the order had earlier study centers in Kentucky and Ohio, nevertheless, it was not until 1905—one hundred years after the inauguration of the American Province of the Order of Preachers—that the Dominican House of Studies in Washington, D.C., was founded as the first intellectual center of the province.

3. Dean Hoge, *The Future of Catholic Leadership: Responses to the Priest Shortage* (Kansas City: Sheed & Ward, 1987) 161–162. Hoge estimates that, if permitted, the number of women entering priesthood would not be enough to make a great impact on the priest shortage.

4. David Power, see next chapter in this collection.

5. W. M. Abbott and J. Gallagher, eds., *The Documents of Vatican II,* "Decree on the Ministry and Life of Priests," *Presbyterorum ordinis,* (New York: Guild Press, 1966) 541, par. 5.

6. *The Documents of Vatican II,* "Dogmatic Constitution on the Church," *Lumen gentium,* 60, par. 34.

7. Raymond E. Brown, *Priest and Bishop: Biblical Reflections* (Paramus, N.J.: Paulist, 1970) 13; cf. Y. Congar, *Lay People in the Church* (Westminster, Md.: Newman, 1957) 112–221.

8. Christian Duquoc, *Christologie: Essai dogmatique; Vol. I—L'Homme Jesus* (Paris: Les Editions du Cerf, 1968), 211.

9. Ibid., 213.

10. *The Documents of Vatican II*, "Decree on the Appropriate Renewal of the Religious Life," *Perfectae caritatis*, 467, par. 1.

11. *Lumen gentium*, 66–67, par. 40.

12. *Perfectae caritatis*, 467, par. 1.

13. Ibid., 468, par. 2b.

14. Ibid., 466, par. 1; 476–477, par. 14.

15. *The Documents of Vatican II*, "Dogmatic Constitution on Divine Revelation," *Dei verbum*, 113, par. 4 .

16. John Paul II, *Post-Synodal Apostolic Exhortation, Christifideles Laici*, Vatican Translation (Boston: Daughters of St. Paul, 1989), 88, par. 35; 84, par. 34.

17. Ibid., 30f, par. 14.

18. *Perfectae caritatis*, 470–471, par. 6.

Representing Christ in Community and Sacrament

David N. Power, O.M.I.

This paper is addressed to the relation of the ordained minister to Christ and to the Church. Its point of departure is found in the phrases *in persona Christi* and *in persona Ecclesiae*. These are the phrases that in Thomistic theology, and later in magisterial teaching, are used to distinguish the role of the ordained minister in the Church from that of the baptized.

A reconsideration of the import of these expressions seems opportune in the light of the teaching on the Church and ministry of the Second Vatican Council, the implementation of liturgical reforms, and some of the concerns of John Paul II as he addresses the role of the priest and the relation of priest to the mission of the laity. In order to focus the reconsideration from the outset, the topic may be defined as follows: What is the role of the ordained minister in mediating the presence and salvific action of Christ in the Church and in its worship and in giving apt symbolic expression to that presence?

To elaborate on the topic, one first has to look at history to see exactly how the term *in persona Christi* originated and what was intended by it, as well as by the term *in persona Ecclesiae*, when this is employed of the priest. The theology of Saint

Thomas Aquinas is particularly important on this score.[1] One
can then ask how the understanding of order is affected when
it is set in the context of recent magisterial and theological
developments, from which new issues and concerns arise.

In Persona Christi

The phrase has its origins in the scriptural exegesis prac-
ticed by early Christian writers. The original form was, in
Latin *ex persona* and in the Greek equivalent, *apo prosopou*. The
particular purpose in using it was to attribute specific words
to a given person in the interpretation of a biblical text. Thus,
in the exegesis of Psalm 2, certain words are attributed to
Christ, others to God the Father who anoints Jesus as his Son,
others to the apostles, and others to the psalmist who admires
the mystery of Christ's defeat of the nations who battle against
God's reign.

It is in the exegesis of 2 Corinthians 2:10, according to
the version of the Vulgate, that the foundation is laid for the
sacramental use of the term *in persona Christi*. The English
translation of the Vulgate reads: "What I have pardoned, if
I pardoned anything, for your sakes have I done it in the person of Christ." The original Greek text does not, of course,
refer to an official ecclesial act of pardon, and the phrase is
more properly translated "in the presence of Christ" than
"in the person of Christ." Nonetheless, Church writers went
by the words *in persona Christi* and read the text as an official
pardon of sins by Paul, in virtue of the power given him by
Christ.[2]

When the term was adopted in the Middle Ages, it was
given a more specific use and applied to a variety of sacramental rites in order to underline specific actions or words, indicating that these are the precise words or actions in which
in the assembly Christ acts through the ordained minister.
It is the assurance of Christ's action in the liturgy, especially
his sanctifying action, that is at stake. The assurance that

Christ acts through the Church's ministers was extended also
to those teachings which were offered, in virtue of episcopal
authority, as the authentic word of Jesus Christ. In either case,
we see that it is the formal act or word of the ordained minister
that is intended, those moments when in the Church he performs those central acts of the Church's worship that are sanctifying, or those wherein he formulates the apostolic witness
and the Church's belief. Sometimes, too, the phrase was extended to include all those official acts whereby the bishop
acted as head of the Church, emphasizing the point that such
authority is a power given by Christ and not a human authority earned by the bishop in his own person.

Saint Thomas Aquinas[3]

St. Thomas Aquinas was ready to use the term *in persona
Christi* both of the activity of the bishop as chief pastor, having power over the mystical body, and of the action of the
ordained priest in the sacraments when he speaks in the first
person singular. This was particularly important in the Eucharistic consecration, when Christ's own words are pronounced.
An analogous importance was attached by Thomas to the
words said by the priest in the first person singular in giving
absolution or conferring baptism. Though these are not directly Christ's words, they do express what the priest does
precisely as Christ's instrument, in virtue of the power of the
sacramental character. Thus, for Thomas Aquinas, the phrase
means to have power from Christ to act in such a way that
one's acts are the acts of Christ.[4]

In the case of the power of the bishop over the Church,
exercised in teaching and in jurisdiction, his vision of hierarchy is influenced by the writings of the Pseudo-Dionysius on
the ecclesiastical hierarchy. He highlights the role of the bishop
in sanctifying the people, according to the divine dispensation whereby the world is ordered in its varied ranks. It is
thus the headship of the bishop and the power he has to govern

the Church and sanctify the people that is expressed when Thomas says that the bishop as bishop acts in the person of Christ. Thus it means practically the same thing as *gerere vicem Christi*, when what is intended is the exercise of the power of Christ who is head of the mystical body.

The profound reason for the unity of the Church with Christ in worship is given by Saint Thomas when he expresses the unity effected by Christ's redemptive act: "Sicut naturale corpus est unum, ex membrorum diversitate consistens, ita tota Ecclesia, quae est mysticum corpus Christi computatur quasi una persona cum suo capite, quod est Christus" (S. Th. 3,49,1,c). In other words, it is the communion in grace between Christ and the Church, on which Thomas elaborates in the question on the grace of Christ's headship (cf. 3,8), that constitutes the basis for understanding ecclesial worship. For Aquinas, the communion effected by Christ's passion is not a mere abstract consideration. It is something won by Christ through his deeds. Though the incarnation and hence the dignity of Christ's person is the foundation of his redemptive power, Thomas accentuates the immensity of the love shown by him for humans and the excess of his suffering (S.Th. 3,48,2,c). Thus, in describing the sacrifice of Christ, he takes up the definition given by Augustine (*De civitate Dei* X, 6) wherein the purpose of sacrifice is given as the bringing together of persons into one communion in God (S. Th. 3,48,3,c).

Despite this fundamental unity, however, Aquinas prefers a somewhat restrictive use of the phrase *in persona Christi* when he employs it of the sacraments. To give fuller expression to the action of the ordained minister in the liturgy, he allies it with the phrase *in persona Ecclesiae*. Following on the idea that "to act in the person of another" is to have authority from the other and to act in virtue of that authority, Aquinas explains that to act in the sacrament in the person of Christ is to be Christ's instrument.[5] The term gives meaning to the words and actions predicated of the first person, when the priest says "I" or "my," as though it were Christ speaking. In these words and actions, the priest acts as instrument of Christ, consecrating, absolving, sanctifying, and the like. To borrow a phrase from some contemporary authors, these are the downward actions of Christ's humanity and mediation, those by which he brings the power of God to act in the community.[6]

There are two cases in which, according to Aquinas, the minister acts *in persona Ecclesiae.* The first is in the profession of faith. Acts of worship for Thomas are by their nature protestations or professions of faith. When faith is lacking in the recipient, as in the case of an infant candidate for baptism, or when it is deficient on the part of others involved, as may be the case with the child's sponsors, the faith of the Church as expressed by the minister supplies this faith.[7] Apparently, this profession of faith in the person or name of the Church can also be made by the nonordained. This is probably what Thomas had in mind when he associated the public profession of faith with the character of confirmation.[8]

The second case in which the minister acts in the person of the Church is more important and universal. It has to do with his duty to express the devotion and worship of the Church as a body, especially in the offering of its spiritual sacrifice. Besides professing ecclesial faith, worship is intended to unite the Church with Christ in devotion and reverence toward God. That worship is expressed by the ordained minister when, as such, he offers prayers of homage and intercession to God. Hence his action *in persona Ecclesiae* is a cultic action wherein the Church's devotion and spiritual sacrifice is expressed.[9] This distinguishes the action of the Church in giving homage from its action, through a minister, as instrument of Christ's sanctifying power, though the latter properly occurs in the context of the former. To illustrate this, we can see what happens in the case of the excommunicated priest who consecrates the species.[10] The action of Christ is in effect cut off from the action of the Church as a communion in faith, rendering homage to God through Christ. There is the abnormal situation that while the priest performs the act, representative of the immolation of Christ in which the sacrifice of the Church is normally perfected, he does not in this case *offer* the sacrifice of the Church. In other words, the sacrifice of Christ may well be represented in the consecration, but this memorial does not become the sacrifice of the Church unless offered in the communion of faith and grace whereby it is one mystical person with Christ.

What is implied in all of this is a distinction between those actions and prayers made by the Church as instrument of sanctification, in which the Church's faith embraces the dispensation of salvation, and those performed by it as actions done in virtue of the grace of communion and intended to render worthy worship to God as a people that in spiritual offerings joins itself as one person with its head, Christ. To use the contemporary terminology already mentioned, this is the upward movement of worship.[11] Both kinds of actions, however, require the mediation of the ordained minister acting either in the person of Christ or in the person of the Church.

Thomas Viewed in the Light of History

In all of this, Thomas Aquinas' view of the ministerial action of the priest seems to allow for two distinctions not prevalent in the vision of an earlier age. First of all, he distinguishes the instrumental acts of the priest from the other acts of ecclesial worship. Second, he sets the action and prayer of the priest in contrast with the action and prayer of the Church as a body of believers.

For earlier liturgies and writers, it is in the entire action of blessing and rite, performed in virtue of leadership in the community, that the representation of Christ and of Christ's mysteries is located. Though at times, as for example in Saint

Ambrose,[12] special attention is given to the repetition of the
exact words of Christ at the Supper, these are not taken out
of the prayer context to which they belong. The grace whereby
Christ and members form one body or, as it were, one person means that the prayer of Christ and the prayer of the
Church are inseparable. Christ's mystery is represented in
the liturgy as ecclesial action because this is the prayer of the
body, head and members, and it is in and through this ecclesial action that the sanctifying power of Christ's Spirit is at
work. Though some prayers and actions were clearly considered to be more vital and important than others, one does
not find the distinction found in Thomas between actions performed in the person of Christ and actions performed in the
person of the Church.

The Eastern Churches arrived at a more felicitous expression of the mystery of the body and its prayer because of their
use of the epiclesis for the Spirit. This shows that it is the transforming power of the Spirit that weds Christ and faithful
together into one body, as it is the Spirit who turns the prayer
and ritual of the body into a life-giving action. After
Augustine, whose sacramentology includes the role of the
Spirit, the West was unable to find as clear a way of expressing the unity of Christ with the Church, and of his action in
the Church. The preference was for more institutional and
juridical formulae.

There are, of course, passages in early Church writers in
which the action of the bishop or priest is more specifically
related to Christ and explained as Christ's action. Thus, Saint
Cyprian, in *Letter 63*, finds that when the bishop proclaims
the prayer of blessing, he takes the place of Christ and offers
the passion of Christ.[13] Cyprian apparently finds that what
the Eucharist renews is the Supper, which stands to the cross
as *passio* to *immolatio*, as self-offering to bloody death. He states
that in the prayer (i.e., the Eucharistic Prayer) that sanctifies the bread and wine, the offering of Christ is renewed,
the offering of the Church being included in it, as the water

in the wine. In other words, it is the renewal of Christ's Supper action in the Church, so as to include the Church, that is the sacramental significance of the priest's (bishop's) oblation.

Among early Church writers, Saints John Chrysostom and Augustine are among those who most emphatically stressed that the actions of the bishop or priest in the sacraments are the actions of Christ. According to Chrysostom, when in baptism the faithful see the priest touch the head of the candidate, "our spiritual eyes see the great High Priest as he stretches forth his invisible hand to touch the head [of the candidate]."[14] This is linked with the action of the Spirit of the risen Christ, for elsewhere Chrysostom says, "It is not a man who does what is done, but it is the grace of the Spirit which sanctifies the nature of the water and touches your head together with the hand of the priest."[15] In such passages, what is being explained is that in the sacraments of the Church, as performed by bishops and presbyters, who are called priests, it is Christ and the Spirit of Christ who are at work. Because the role of the Spirit is kept to the fore, it is clear that Christ's sanctifying action belongs within the communion of the Church, Christ's body, or, as Augustine puts it, the sacrifice of head and members.[16]

These considerations may best be grasped in relation to the Eucharistic Prayer, which as a prayer of blessing and memorial is the paradigm for all ecclesial blessing. While in virtue of the Supper narrative and memorial command, the prayer is referred back to Christ's words and actions at the Supper itself, the texts of the prayers indicate that what is deemed to be represented is the transformation of humanity and of human nature in the flesh of Christ, the re-creation of the human race.[17] It is Christ who contains within himself the whole of humanity, who is present in the liturgy. It is transformed humanity, as represented by the Church, that joins with him in the blessing of God and at the table where all flesh is made whole and immortal through the power of the

Body and Blood. What the priest does in the blessing is to express how Christ and Church are together united as the new creation, and it is through participation in this one body that individuals are sanctified.

In keeping with such considerations, we can see that in fact the deepest and most important intuition of Aquinas lies in the perception that Christ and Church through redemption are, as it were, but one person. In signaling this communion, in bringing forward the images of satisfaction and sacrifice that express his solidarity with sinful humanity, Thomas is ever mindful of the immensity of his love and the intensity of his pain, whereby he draws all persons to himself. It is not a purely juridical unity that is effected but one that is gained in this truly personal way. But in the distinctions that he makes between the acts of the minister and the actions of the people, between those done in the person of Christ and those done in the person of the Church, he subordinates this insight to a more hierarchical and instrumental view of the role of the ordained.

When Saint Thomas considers the holiness required of bishop or presbyter in his treatment of the states of life, he appeals in the first place to the pastoral charge (*cura animarum*), which they assumed. In a reflection of the state of things in his time, it is interesting to note that he distinguishes between the dedication of the bishop's whole life to the ministry (S. Th. 2-2,184,6,c) and the presbyter's part-time dedication (2-2,184,8,c). In both cases, the care of souls carries with it an obligation to live a devout life. Since the bishop is the shepherd of souls, he must be ready to give up his life for his sheep. Following Pseudo-Dionysius, Thomas further remarks that the duty to enlighten others carries with it the duty to be enlightened oneself (1.c). As far as the presbyter is concerned, while the care of souls compels holiness of life, this is required even more of him by the service of the altar, where he serves Christ himself: "ipsi Christo servitur in sacramento altaris, ad quod requiritur maior sanctitas interior

quam requirat etiam religionis status'' (2-2, 184, 8, c). In the
article quoted, Saint Thomas applies this reasoning also to
the archdeacon.

From Aquinas to Trent

In Thomas' own time, there were those who sought to reform the life of the clergy by appealing to the priest's relation to Christ, both in preaching and in sacrament, and to
the need for him to give good example to the faithful. In a
special way, they found that they could draw inspiration from
his duty to celebrate the sacrifice of the Mass. Thus, William
Durand in the admonition to candidates to the presbyterate,
which he inserted into the *Pontifical*, exhorted them to imitate the mysteries that they performed in a life of holiness and
chastity.[18] It was also the call on the priest to offer the sacrifice
for others that put a greater demand of sanctity on him. In
medieval times, people had frequent resort to monks to plead
their prayers, often in connection with the mutations in the
penitential system, where fervent prayer could substitute for
the doing of penance. Later this seemed to devolve on the
priest, to whom it belonged to pray the Church's prayer in
the Divine Office and to offer the Mass for the living and the
dead. As one who intercedes, his communion with Christ
ought to be all the more evident. Curiously, therefore, the
actions that according to Thomas were performed in the person of the Church had the effect in practical piety of associat-
ing him all the more fully with Christ. One could say that
the idea that he acted in the person of Christ, though it was
given a very restrictive sense by Aquinas, tended to absorb
all the actions of the ordained minister when appeal was made
to his affinity with Christ as the basis for his spirituality.

This was the idea to which reformers of the clergy had
resort when such reform was greatly needed, leading up to
the time of the Protestant Reformation and after it. It became
an integral part of what we can broadly call the Catholic Refor-

mation, or the Tridentine Reform.[19] From a situation, then, in which the term *in persona Christi* had a very specific and clearly circumscribed meaning, there was a move to see the priest as one who had a special relation with Christ, operative not only in (all) his ministerial actions but also in his personal life. In more recent centuries, this ideal has had a large influence on the preparation of the clergy, due to the influence of Saint-Sulpice. Much discretion needs to be used in attributing ideas about the priesthood to the members of this school and society, but there is no denying the influence of Cardinal Berulle's identification of priesthood with sacrifice and hence his spirituality of priestly identity with the high priest, Jesus Christ.[20]

Ordination and Women[21]

For Aquinas, the significance and beauty of the sacrament of orders lies in the fact that it meshes with the way in which God influences and directs all his works. As in all things according to the law of nature, God orders his dispensations by having some creatures order others, so in the Church he exercises the power of sanctification on all through the ministry of some. Those who are ordained to confer the sacraments, or in the case of the bishop to govern the Church, represent God's eminence and influence (Suppl. 34,1).

It is on these grounds that Thomas excludes women from ordination. Because of the natural and social relations between male and female, Thomas does not find it fitting to ordain women. It is not in the nature of things that they should exercise public office and leadership: "cum in sexu femineo non possit significari aliqua eminentia gradus, quia mulier statum subiectionis habet" (S. Th., Suppl. 39,1,c). He knows that women can be more gifted and more virtuous than men, but in that case the order of nature, rather than anything specific to the Christian order, requires that they exercise their influence over others in a private, not in a public, setting.

He says this despite the fact that in his own time some women held regal sway over kingdoms and principalities. He appears to think that what might be acceptable in the temporal order is in no way acceptable in the spiritual, where the hierarchy of nature and of divine order is to be constantly respected.

It is clearly a specific notion of gender differences that determines the case of women's ordination for Aquinas, and it goes with his specific notion that the ordained minister is vicar and representative of Christ's power or headship over the Church. It is not a mere historical fact that ordination requires masculine sex, but a historical fact that was itself in keeping with the order of nature, whereby the male exercises leadership and the woman practices subjection.

This last point was made much more specific by Bonaventure, when he ruled out the ordination of women (Sent. 4,d.25,a.2,q.1), with important reference to an understanding of God's relation to creation and to the Church. He sees this as a masculine-feminine relation, basing his notion on a gender differentiation that sees the masculine as active and the feminine as passive (Sent. 2,d.18,a.1,q.1). Since the ordained minister must represent God's action in the Church, it is necessary that the minister be male. The relation for Bonaventure is not directly to the incarnate Word but to the nature of God and of God's creative relation to the world.

It took Scotus[22] to bypass the question of fittingness or symbolism and simply appeal to the positive fact of God's ordinance that the Word take on flesh in masculine form, and Christ's ordinance that males exercise the priesthood in the Church. However, one does have to recognize that a comparable kind of institutional reasoning is already at work in the sacramental theology of Thomas Aquinas. In such matters as the number of the sacraments, or the precise matter and form of sacraments, he always turns to some specific determination by Christ to settle the point. He is always concerned to link this with reasons of "necessity" or fittingness, but his vision of the origins of the Church, its offices, powers,

and sacraments, is one that finds these origins in an institution by Christ, conveyed to the apostles. It is the Scotist tradition, however, that turns this into a simple matter of positive
divine will and divine freedom.

What would happen to Thomas' historical determinism
if it were to be proved that the facts were otherwise, or to his
secure sense that things are as they are if the fittingness on
further consideration proved unfitting? How much does the
assuredness of things historically determined depend on the
appearance of fittingness, and how much is the fittingness
simply tailored to fit the order given? Rather than seeing one
come before the other, it is the interplay between perceived
meaning and historical interpretation that calls for attention.
This is always the case in historical interpretation, where the
relation to presuppositions and experiences cannot be gainsaid.

Recent Statements of the Magisterium

A word needs to be said about recent magisterial use of
the terms *in persona Christi* and *in persona Ecclesiae*. In the en-
cyclical *Mediator Dei* Pius XII used it in the strong Thomistic
sense of delineating an action performed by the priest in virtue of a specific character and power received from Christ.[23]
He extended it, however, beyond the formal sacramental action to cover the entire liturgical presidency of the priest, so
that he could say that it is in virtue of his action in the person
of Christ that the priest also acts in the person of the Church,
especially in offering the Eucharistic sacrifice.

The Second Vatican Council retrieved what can be considered a more patristic view of worship. The Constitution
on the Sacred Liturgy, in noting the various modes of Christ's
presence in the liturgy, noted in the first place the presence
of Christ in the priest who offers the Eucharistic sacrifice, and
principally his presence in the sacramental species (*Sacrosanctum concilium* 7). This was, however, completed by noting the
presence in the word and in the Church's common prayer.

When norms for liturgical reform were given, the hierarchical nature of the liturgy was seen to be completed by the nature of the liturgy as the communal action of all. This does place the presence of Christ through the priest and in the sacramental species in the context of his presence by faith and the power of the Spirit in the body of the faithful or, in other words, in the Church as body of Christ, joined with him as one body through faith and the Holy Spirit. Quite interestingly, in the postconciliar document *Eucharisticum mysterium* on the implementation of the constitution, it was the presence of Christ in the congregation that was first noted, as the context in which the special presence through the minister is verified.[24] Neither document uses the terminology *in persona*. Hence they do not settle the meaning of these terms nor the theological questions underlining the usage.

The Decree on the Ministry and Life of Priests in its second paragraph uses the term *in persona Christi Capitis*, while in the very same paragraph emphasizing that the sacrament and character of order are rooted in the baptismal character and that the priesthood of the ordained is in service of the priesthood of the faithful (*Presbyterorum ordinis* 2). Later on, the document repeats the phrase *in persona Christi*, without addition, when it mentions the priest's sacramental ministry (12). In looking for the right expression to use in order to express the presbyter's relation to Christ, the council members were also concerned about finding a foundation for priestly spirituality. This needed to be one that would not appear to derogate from the call to follow Christ of all the baptized. It also needed to include a focus on the priest's pastoral and apostolic ministries, rather than uniquely on his Eucharistic celebration of Christ's sacrifice. Inserting the word *Capitis* alongside *in persona Christi* both highlighted the relation of the ordained minister to the whole body, in its call to serve Christ and the gospel, and allowed for the inclusion of all the services that the priest exercised in the Church. When in paragraph 12 the decree lays down the foundation for the spiritual life of the priest, it states that he has been configured through ordination to "Christ the priest as servant of the head," and that he is the instrument of Christ the priest in the service of the Church and the restoration of the human race to God's grace. In the context, the sacrifice of Christ is presented as his loving service, and the image of the servant complements the image of the eternal priest.

An interesting twist to the idea of taking the place of Christ is given in the postconciliar instruction on the restoration of the Divine Office as the communal prayer of the Church. In that document, it is said that the bishop and the presbyter take the place of Christ even as they offer the prayer of the Church, since even while praying the Office with others they are joined with Christ in his supplication for the people.[25] This is to fortify the distinction between the ordained and the laity in all Church actions, even when together they offer the same prayer as a common action.

We find that in some texts of John Paul II, the term *in persona Christi* recurs to highlight the distinction between the sacramental action of the priest in representing Christ's sacrifice and the spiritual action of the faithful in uniting themselves with it.[26] Here it has a meaning very close to that found in Thomas Aquinas, being used to accentuate the instrumental and representative nature of the priest's liturgical action. On the other hand, in the postsynodal document on the laity, *Christifideles laici*, the Pope uses the expression from the decree on priests, *in persona Christi Capitis*, and says that the power of the ordained is to "gather the Church in the Holy Spirit, through the Gospel and the Sacraments."[27] This is to take the reference to the headship of Christ over the Church as a way of underscoring the mission of the priest to the faithful in the ministry of word and sacrament.

When Pope John Paul explains the exclusion of women from ordination, he refers to the 1976 statement of the Congregation for the Doctrine of the Faith, saying that this is not an issue of dignity but of function. He gives the same reason for ordaining only men as the Congregation, namely, that "this is a practice that the church has always found in the expressed will of Christ, totally sovereign and free."[28] However, he adds a note of fittingness to the practice when he says that it "can be understood from the rapport between Christ, the Spouse, and his Bride, the Church."

In the documents *Mulieris dignitatem*[29] and *Christifideles laici*, John Paul II speaks strongly against discrimination against women, in society and in the Church. He offers a reading of Genesis that brings out the nature of the human in the unity of male and female, a unity in equality, without natural subordination. He clearly wishes to go beyond patriarchy and to emphasize a unity of the sexes in love and coresponsibility. When he speaks of society, he envisages an equality of both sexes and clearly sees the role of women in positions even of the highest leadership. At the same time, some gender differentiation is clearly at work in his thought. The Pope does say that women and men, by reason of their distinctive natures, have different kinds of contributions to make to Church and society. What he underlines in the case of women is the call to motherhood and what he sees as a feminine sensitivity to the human person, not encountered in the male.

When it comes to his theology of Church, however, he is fond of the imagery of bridegroom and bride to express the relation of Christ to the Church, and vice versa. He also appeals to the specific will of Christ to call only men to the company of the twelve apostles as the reason for excluding women from ordination, even as he gives much importance to the ministry whereby they serve the Church in equality with men. Behind this positive ordinance, there is the theology of the Church that makes appeal to the imagery of a relationship between bride and bridegroom to express the relation between the Church and Christ. For the Pope, this requires that in the Eucharist itself the diversification be kept between male and female and that Christ be represented by the man in relation to the female image of the Church.[30] The argument from the bride-bridegroom imagery is of course allied in the work of Pope John Paul II with a strong distinction in worship between the action of the priest and the action of the baptized, between the instrumental action of the priest in sacrament and the people's spiritual participation in the mystery that is represented.

The Question Reconsidered

In all of this recent magisterial teaching, we find the invitation to consider more fully the way in which the ordained minister represents both the salvific action of Christ and the prayer of the Church, as well as the function of the priest in building up the church through his ministry to the baptized in word and sacrament. It is only within that broader context that arguments for the exclusive candidacy of males can be considered, though naturally what is said on that score affects the whole question. The fundamental issue in a theology of ministry is the way in which the relation of the ordained to the baptized is considered.

In the case of Saint Thomas Aquinas, the exclusion of women seemed fitting because of man's natural social superiority and his ideas about God's governance of the world. For Bonaventure, the symbols of God's action in the world needed to be masculine because of the nature of the creative act. While he sets aside such considerations, Pope John Paul II corroborates his reading of the scriptural ordinance with the redemptive symbolism of bride and bridegroom, which leads him to the conviction that the ordained minister has to be male in order to represent Christ the bridegroom. Not only is this because Christ was a male but because the union of male and female itself deserves this diversification in liturgy. All three reasonings just mentioned suppose that there is one set of actions wherein the priest represents the sanctifying act of Christ and another set wherein he represents the prayer of the

Church. Despite the use of the bride-bridegroom imagery, it is never suggested that this latter requires a female representative, and that itself raises a question about distinguishing these two kinds of action. More fundamental than the exclusion of women from order, then, is that of the relation between minister and community in all activities of the Church, and most particularly in sacrament and worship. It is to be asked whether it is not possible to see a unity, a oneness between Christ's action and that of the body, that overcomes the kind of differentiation that seems to hold the priest apart from the body.

One cue is found in Saint Thomas himself, in his image of Christ and Church as one person. There is perhaps another cue in the phrase adopted by John Paul II, that to act in the person of Christ the head of the Church is to gather the Church together in the Spirit through the gospel and through the sacraments. The church is to be bound together in the communion of the Spirit, but it is also to be bound together in its prayer as the body of Christ and in giving the witness of humankind's reconciliation to the world (*Lumen gentium* 1). It seems possible to pursue this issue of priestly representation by joining more closely together what is traditionally signified by the term *in persona Christi* with what is traditionally signified by *in persona Ecclesiae*. The twist given to the phrase in the expression *in persona Christi Capitis* would then have to do with gathering the baptized, through obedience to the gospel, into the one sacramental action, which is that of Christ and his body, the Church, or of Christ living through the Spirit in the body. The diversification between the role of the baptized and the role of the ordained would still be clear, but in relation to the one ecclesial action rather than in relation to distinct acts within the one action.

As we saw, the Second Vatican Council placed the role of the priest in his relationship to Christ in the broader context of the action of the Church as Christ's body. Much recent sacramental theology has retrieved a broader notion of sacrament, so that it is possible to see the sacramental actions of the Church, body and community, as manifestations of the presence of the risen Christ in the Church and in the world. The difficulty with the medieval theology encapsulated in the term *in persona Christi* was that it separated the sanctifying action of Christ in the Church and, through the expressed faith of the Church, from its homage to God in Christ. To use another terminology, one could say that it separated the descending act of God in Christ from the ascending act of Christ in the Church. Eventually, even the phrase *in persona Ecclesiae* seemed to have the same effect.

The Vatican Council underlines that the action of the body united in faith and grace with Christ is the action of Christ. One could say in line with this that the sanctifying and worshipful action of Christ in the Church is the action of the Church itself as a believing community, when it is united by the ordained ministry. The glorified Christ is totally one with the body, or Christ and Church are united as one body, what Augustine called the *totus Christus*. Even the spousal imagery of Ephesians 5 in the end feeds into this image of the one body, according to the Genesis image of *Adam* as one person, male and female, no longer two but one.

This imagery is mentioned because there is another way of putting the question than that of accentuating the male-female distinction. In the redemption of humanity, is Christ, in his dying and rising, to be seen as the male unit of a renewed male-female unity in one body? Or is Christ the recapitulation of the renewed *human*, in which from one point of view male and female together constitute the *one*, and in which from another "there is neither male nor female"? Through the Spirit, Christ is in the whole Church as a body without distinction, and the whole Church without distinction is in Christ. Or, in other words, Jesus Christ through the metamorphosis of his death, descent into Hades, and resurrection represents redeemed humanity in its solidarity. This cannot be captured if one insists on male-female distinctions or if one employs

the terminology of headship in such a way as to accentuate
the historical maleness of Christ. Though in his historical existence Jesus Christ was indeed a male, this was the submission of the divine Word and Wisdom to the limiting conditions
of human enfleshment. On the one hand, it was by the very
surrender to these limiting conditions, culminating in a death
that gave divine testimony against all evil and negative limi-
tation, that Jesus established his total solidarity with the whole
human race. On the other hand, when raised up from the
dead and made Lord, Jesus Christ was transformed by the
Spirit in such a way that he takes body in the Church in the
communion in which there is neither male nor female, Jew
nor Greek, slave nor free. While the outflow of grace is the
exercise of his headship, it is expressed in the Church in the
unity of Christ with his members as one body, the whole
Christ. The actions of Christ in the Church are the actions
of the body, or, there is only one action, which is that of the
body, head and members, as though one person.

    This leads us to ask what exactly it is that the ordained
minister represents when acting as minister of the assembly.
Is it some action of a historical Jesus from the past, or is it
the oneness of the body in Christ, the action of Christ in this
body, the community of a reconciled and transformed humanity? It would seem that what is more expressly signified in
the prayers and actions of the presiding minister is the effect
of Christ's mediation, and the reality of the communion of
head and members as one, as this was brought about through
the deeds commemorated.

Symbolic Representation

    Symbolic or sacramental representation does not mean a
figurative imitation of the events and acts commemorated and
now effective. Often enough in the course of history, such ex-
planation has been attempted, no doubt because it is a sim-
pler way. Commemoration, however, has more to do with

a recall that signifies the meaning and present repercussion of what is remembered. It is formulated through narrative, blessing, and ritual. It is of the understanding of the ritual actions of commemoration that we need to be particularly careful, since it is these and their actors that are most easily seen as figuratively representing past acts or invisible agents, especially when joined with words of declaration. When, however, one properly considers the rites of Christian sacrament, one notes that their immediate referent is always an ecclesial action in the present, not the action of Christ in the past. In other words, the salvific deeds of Christ's Pasch are commemorated in a narrative proclamation that recalls the past as presently efficacious, and in a ritual that represents an ecclesial reality that expresses communion in Christ. These are completed and given form in a blessing, which is the prayer of the body, that arises out of the narrative and comes to bear on the ecclesial rite. Such rites are the common table of bread and wine, Christ's Body and Blood; the incorporation of new members through the bath of cleansing and regeneration, anointing with the Spirit, and invitation to the table of Christ's sacrifice; the welcome back into the community and to the common table of the repentant sinner; the reception of the witness of woman and man that they shall be for the Church the abiding witness of covenant union; the strengthening through prayer and anointing of those who image Christ's sufferings and resurrection hope in their own pain and fidelity. The role of the presiding minister in all of this is to gather the community through gospel and blessing into the common ritual action, either as direct participant or as witness, so that the communion of the Church as the body of Christ and Christ's presence in this communion of Spirit may truly be expressed.

In ancient liturgies, there is no question of the ordained minister speaking words of Christ in the first person, even in the case of the words taken from the Supper narrative. These occur not as an isolated declaration but in the context of a memorial and epiclesis, as a basis for the Church's remembrance in a prayer of thanksgiving and intercession rather than simply in their own right.[31] What the memorial command grounds is thus the prayer that the priest offers in the first person plural, that prayer which he offers as the prayer of the body, Christ praying in and through the members with whom he is completely one in the grace of a communion in the Spirit. Though in the Latin medieval West, the declarative form took over in the other sacraments such as baptism and penance, in earlier times it was the blessing prayer over the water or over the penitents, uttered in the name of the Church, that signified and made efficacious the saving grace of Christ. It is always when the headship of Christ is signified in the communion of one prayer and one ritual, which results from this influence, that grace is offered to individual Church members. One could therefore say that what the ordained presider directly signifies in his prayer and action is the communion in diversity of the body of Christ, and that it is indirectly through this prayer of communion that the headship of Christ is represented and the mystery of salvation commemorated. The proclamatory is inherent in the blessing, rather than distinct from it.

The Sacrament of Order[32]

This interpretation is bolstered by a reflection on the precise significance of the sacrament of order in and for the Church. The sacrament itself is conferred in the assembly of the Church and by the prayer of the Church for the bestowal of the Spirit. What it signifies is the unity of the Church as humanity reconciled in Christ, the openness of each assembly to catholic communion with other communities, and the apostolic tradition in which Christians are united in faith and in witness. These all have the unity of the body as such as primary referent, but because this is a unity in Christ through the Spirit, then it has as secondary referent the headship of

Christ. Moreover, this headship is not to be taken in juridical terms but is an influence won by the love and suffering of his passion, and is now exercised through the outpouring of the Spirit, that same Spirit in which he gave himself over to death.

From this it follows that there is no attempt in liturgical action to figuratively represent or dramatize the past redemptive actions of Christ, though these are indeed commemorated. It is also hard to find a reason for a specific resemblance of the ordained minister to Christ, other than in a common humanity. It is the communion of the Church in Christ, and of Christ present through the efficacious work of the Spirit, represented in the prayers and sacramental actions of the Church, that are united as one through the power and ministry of the ordained. While the reality of Jesus Christ as Jew, Galilean, male, wandering prophet, condemned blasphemer, and crucified criminal is most important to our commemoration of how redemption was effected, these qualities themselves do not bear specific figuration. Indeed, what is represented is how, by this self-exinanition and subjection to the limitations of human existence and witness to God, Jesus was made Lord. It is through the power of the resurrection that he became a life-giving body, ever present in the Church in ways that are always particular but do not allow confinement to any time, place, gender, race, color, or culture.

Conclusions

Three principal conclusions can be drawn from this essay.

First, traditionally and currently, the phrase *in persona Christi* expresses the belief that in some particular liturgical or authoritative act the sanctifying power of Christ is active. Similarly, the phrase *in persona Ecclesiae* signifies another aspect of the priest's action, whereby the prayer of the whole Church is unified in his prayer. As a way of expressing the simultaneous relation of the priest to Christ and to the body of the faithful, some use has been made recently of the phrase *in persona Christi Capitis.* None of these expressions was used in the past to refer specifically to the minister himself, but they envisaged those specific actions that he performed in virtue of ordination. Even when the question of the minister's sex was raised by Thomas Aquinas or Bonaventure, it was a particular understanding of gender differentiation that postulated a male candidate, not a resemblance to Christ. Mention of this resemblance is quite novel in the Church's teachings. Even now, it does not have a central place. This is held by the conviction that there is a positive divine dispensation expressed in the choice of the twelve apostles. While the imagery of bridegroom and bride is used to express the relation of Christ and the Church, it is hardly the only or even the foremost image of this communion.

It is doubtful that prevailing importance needs to be given to the sexual side of this imagery in configuring the Christ-Church or Christ-humanity relationship. Indeed, that could risk undermining the unity that has been established between Christ and the Church through the work of reconciliation. What is foremost in the benefits of redemption is the communion of Christ with humanity and the union of all in the Church, without discrimination, that is restored by Christ. In expressing the presence of Christ that in the gift of the Spirit brings all into one, the ordained minister needs to gather all into the gospel and the sacrament that express this communion. Hence, the second conclusion of the essay is that the theology of order needs to be developed in such a way that it expresses the intimate unity between the action of the priest and the action of the baptized. It is within that unity that the distinctive features of the ordained minister are best appreciated, for then the relation of his role to the body of Christ stands out in clear relief.

When the magisterium teaches that there is a positive divine disposition that only males can be ordained, arguments for its fittingness leave questions open. When this concern looms large, it appears to go with a way of looking at the priest that accentuates his distinction from the baptized. It turns attention away from those communal actions of the Church in its worship in which as a body, unified through ministry, the saving deeds of Christ are represented and the power of the Spirit transforms, in the hope of God's rule and of eternal life in the divine communion. It belongs to the role of the sacramental presider not to be set off from the rest of the Church but to draw the immense diversity of humanity into the one prayer, the one action, the one communion, which is that of the body of Christ in the Spirit, Christ now alive and present in this body, with which he is but one person by reason of the body given and the blood poured out once for all upon the cross.

The third conclusion is that the spiritual life of the ordained minister is not to be based on the celebration of the Eucharist, in distinction from the rest of the ministry to which he is called. A tendency to do this has been noted, even with some basis in the work of Saint Thomas Aquinas but much more strongly developed by the French school of spirituality. In the perspective of the Second Vatican Council, the ministry of the Eucharist is situated in the ministry to the community of believers, along with the ministries of word and pastoral care. It is indeed the central act of the ministry, as it is the central act of the Church itself and of every Christian, because it is the supreme act of Christ's worship, in which he unites the body with himself, as though one person. The role that the ordained minister takes in this sacrament is one with the role that he has in the pastoral ministry. The model for his life is the same as the model for his ministry, namely, the service of Christ to his people in the giving over of his life on their account. The particular use that the Vatican Council's Decree on the Ministry and Life of Priests made of the terminology of *in persona* serves to put this in context.

Notes

1. In the early part of this paper, I am much indebted to Bernard D. Marliangeas, *Clés pour une Théologie du Ministère, In Persona Christi, In Persona Ecclesiae* (Paris: Ed. Beauchesne, 1978).

2. Cf. Marliangeas, 42–46.

3. Ibid., 89–146.

4. Thomas defines the meaning of the term in general: ". . . quicumque aliquid agit in persona alterius, oportet hoc fieri per potestatem ab illo concessam" (*Summa Theologica*, 3,82,1,c).

5. S. Th., 3,64,2,ad 3m; 3,81,3,ad 3m; 3,82,1,ad 2m, ad 4m; 3,82,2,ad 2m; 3,82,5,c; 3,82,5,ad 2m; 3,83,1,ad 1m. The closest Aquinas comes to presenting the priest himself as an image of Christ is in St. Th. 3,83,1,ad 3m: ". . . etim sacerdos gerit imaginem Christi, in cuius persona et virtute verba pronuntiat ad consecrandum. . . . Et ita quodammodo idem est sacerdos et hostia." Even here, however, the accent is on the power that the priest receives from Christ, and on the words that he pronounces, rather than on any personal likeness of the priest to Christ.

6. E.g., I. Dalmais, "Theology of the Liturgical Celebration," in A. Martimort (ed.), *The Church at Prayer*, vol. 1, *Principles of the Liturgy*, trans. M. O'Connell (Collegeville: The Liturgical Press, 1987) 227–280.

7. S. Th. 3,64,8,ad 2m; 3,64,9,c.

8. S. Th. 3,72,5,ad 2m.

9. S. Th. 3,82,6,c; 3,82,7,ad 3m.

10. S. Th. 3,82,7,c, and ad 3m.

11. Dalmais, 1.c.

12. Ambrose, "Sermons on the Sacraments," in *The Awe-Inspiring Rites of Initiation*, ed. Edward Yarnold (Slough: St. Paul Publications, 1971) 133–136.

13. Cyprian, *Letter 63*, in *The Eucharist*, Message of the Fathers of the Church, vol. 7, ed. Daniel Sheerin (Wilmington: Michael Glazier, 1986) 255–268.

14. John Chrysostom, *Baptismal Instructions*, Ancient Christian Writers, vol. 31, trans. P. W. Harkins (New York: Newman, 1963) 164.

15. Ibid., 46f.

16. *De civitate Dei* X, 6. In this chapter, Augustine gives this definition of sacrifice: "A true sacrifice is every work which is done that we may be united to God in a holy fellowship, and which is referred to that final Good in which alone we can be truly blessed." Of the Eucharist, he says: "This is the sacrifice of christians: 'We, though many, are one body in Christ' (1 Cor 10:17), and this is the sacrifice which the church continually celebrates in the sacrament of the altar, known to the faithful, in which

she teaches that she herself is offered in the offering she makes." The translation is taken from *The Eucharist*, ed. Sheerin, 45f.

17. Cf. Louis Ligier, "The Origins of the Eucharistic Prayer: From the Last Supper to the Eucharist," *Studia Liturgica* 9 (1973) 161–185.

18. The ordination rite is found in M. Andrieu, *Le Pontifical de Guillaume Durand*, volume 3 of *Le Pontifical Romain au Moyen Age* (Vatican City: Studi e Testi 88, 1940), Liber 1, cap. XIII, n. 5, pp. 365–367.

19. Of particular interest is Jean-Pierre Massaut, *Jossé Clichtove, l'humanisme et la réforme du clergé*, 2 vols. (Paris: Editions des Belles Lettres, 1968).

20. Cf. Jacques Le Brun, "Le grand siècle de la spiritualité francaise et ses lendemains," in *Dictionnaire de Spiritualité* 5, 917–953.

21. On the treatment of this issue in medieval theology, cf. J. H. Martin, "The Injustice of Not Ordaining Women: a Problem for Medieval Theologians," *Theological Studies* 48 (1987) 303–316. Thomas Aquinas did not arrive at a treatment of order in writing the *Summa*, so the material is taken from the *Supplementum*.

22. On Scotus, cf. Martin, "Injustice of Not Ordaining Women," 310–313. In writing of authors after Scotus, Martin notes that they raised the question of injustice but dismissed it on account of what they took as a positive divine ordinance. Martin does not attend to the fact that injustice need not be willful and conscious discrimination, but can be embodied in the prevailing ideology.

23. Cf. Marliangeas, 231–236.

24. This is in par. 8 of the document. Cf. *Vatican Council II: Conciliar and Post Conciliar Documents*, ed. Austin Flannery (New York: Costello, 1977) 109.

25. "Institutio generalis de liturgia horarum," in *Enchiridion Documentorum Instaurationis Liturgicae*, vol. 1, edited by Reiner Kaczynski (Rome: Marietti, 1976) 2281.

26. E.g., "On the Lord's Supper: Letter on the Mystery and Cult of the Blessed Eucharist," *The Pope Speaks* 25 (1980) 139–164.

27. John Paul II, *The Vocation and the Mission of the Lay Faithful in the Church and in the World* (Washington: USCC, 1988) 22, p. 57.

28. Ibid., 51, p. 152.

29. John Paul II, *On the Dignity and Vocation of Women* (Washington: USCC, 1988).

30. Ibid., 26, pp. 96–98.

31. Ligier, "Origins of the Eucharistic Prayer."

32. Cf. David N. Power, *Ministers of Christ and His Church: A Theology of Priesthood* (London: G. Chapman, 1969).

Intimacy and Priestly Life

Patricia H. Livingston

Years ago, in one of the first workshops I ever did with priests, something happened that I never forgot. The workshop was part of Fr. Vince Dwyer's Ministry to Priests program, a program for renewal and support for priests. We were in a large, lovely diocese on a coast. Most of the men attending were from that diocese and were the leaders, the ones who would form the team that would carry out the program. They were cultured and witty, articulate and lively. In the midst of them there was a Trappist monk who had come from his abbey to see whether or not he thought the program had possibilities for the monks. He wore his Cistercian habit with sandals on his bare feet. He spoke little, being unaccustomed to conversation. Sitting next to him in the chapel one day, I noticed out of the corner of my eye a flash of blue. It stood out because his robes were all tones of the earth. When I looked more closely I discovered that it was a watch—big and round on a wide plastic strap. The face of it was Charlie Tuna! Later I asked him about it. He smiled shyly and told me the story. He had not been out of the monastery since the 1930s. In the monastery they do not need watches because they tell the time by bells. The whole day is divided into periods of prayer, and the bells mark the progression of the days and nights. He knew when he was coming for this workshop that he would need to know what time it was. Schedules would be more complex. He had gone to ask the Father Abbot for a watch, and the Abbot had opened a drawer and taken out a whole box of promotional watches donated by the tuna fish company.

The image of that priest has stayed with me all these years. The medieval habit and the garish promo watch. The meeting of the worlds. In the middle of the week there was an afternoon off. More than anything the monk wanted to go to the ocean. His monastery was in the Midwest, and he had never been to the coast. He told me on the drive to the beach how strange it was to be in the world after forty years, seeing so many things he had never seen: station wagons and fast-food places and automatic crossing lights and kids with jam boxes.

We parked the car and walked down a hill to a row of dunes. The path cut through the last dune, and suddenly there was the sea. Brilliant blue with huge waves building, holding, shining, it exploded in white and surged to the shore. He fell on his knees and wept. We stayed there a long time in silence, letting it surround us.

On the way back he still did not speak, but from time to time he would touch his watch, the face of the great ocean creature, Charlie, and smile.

I tell that story for two reasons. When Donald Goergen first asked me to write a chapter in a book on priesthood there came to me the faces and voices and presence of so many priests from my workshops over the last twelve years, the stories of so many lives, the vignettes of struggle and beauty. Clear among those presences was the monk with the watch.

The other reason I tell it is that I think it is a metaphor. In so many ways the priesthood is a way of life from ancient times. Not literally robed in garments from earlier centuries as the monk was, priests are nonetheless robed psychologically and spiritually in traditions and behaviors, expectations and regulations, from cultures infinitely removed from our current one.

In the last two years as associate director of the Center
for Continuing Formation in Ministry at the University of
Notre Dame, and for ten years before that in workshops and
retreats and gatherings, I have encountered thousands of
priests. I have been in dioceses and religious communities,
in parishes and on campuses, in seminaries and mission sta-
tions. I have been privileged to be a listener to the hearts of
many priests.

One of the great honors has been that I have been allowed
to witness great graced moments of discovery not unlike the
monk first seeing the ocean and falling to his knees. But more
often than the experience of the inbreaking of beauty, it has
been the experience of the inbreaking of human love.

What I am going to try to do in these pages is to say some
things about intimacy in the lives of priests. Some are things
I have learned from the behavioral sciences. All are things
I have seen confirmed repeatedly in interactions with the lives
of priests. On many occasions in my workshops my teaching
has turned into learning for me, my theories have been illuminated and expanded, challenged and deepened, by their
experience. The truth has become clear to me: Intimacy is
essential in the life of a priest. It is central for personal integration, for ministry, for spirituality.

Integration

The term "intimacy" often connotes romantic involvement or is used as a euphemism for genital sexuality. While
either of these can be sometimes an aspect of intimacy, the
sense in which I will be using the term will follow the usage
of Erik Erikson. He sees intimacy as a power or skill learned
in adult development, a flexible strength for being close to
another. It is "the capacity to commit oneself to concrete affiliations and partnerships and to develop the ethical strength

to abide by such commitments even though they may call for significant sacrifice and compromise.''[1]

From the perspective of personal integration, intimacy is an essential task on the road to full adulthood. Erik Erikson, Carol Gilligan, and Abraham Maslow spell this out in fundamental writings of behavioral science. Evelyn and James Whitehead describe it in *Christian Life Patterns* as ''those strengths which enable a person to share deeply with another.''[2] Intimacy involves personal disclosure and mutuality.

The truth that these works express is that as a person I cannot become fully who I am, a human adult, until I have relationships that involve sustained closeness. I need to have affiliations that employ mutual peer give-and-take; partnerships in which I risk and receive, in which I know another deeply and allow myself to be known in a climate of honesty and trust. It is in this milieu that my private stretchings, my solitary self-understandings are tested. My self-image, the interwoven strands of messages about myself from childhood, are brought into the light of another's experience of me.

This is most precarious. If I am known and who I am is seen as bad or ugly or laughable, I may stagger under the blow of that judgment for years. However, if I am known and who I am is seen as good, as beautiful, as dear, then I will bloom. The voices of self-hatred and self-doubt are confronted by the voices of acceptance and affirmation from the other.

Not everything I will learn about myself is positive. In the climate of the support and care of intimate relationship, deficiencies in me are also revealed. Arrogances and blindnesses, immaturities and lazinesses are uncovered as the exchanges of everyday living progress. I am able to look at unfavorable aspects of myself because I have the foundation of experiences of deep acceptance and respect. I do not need to defend against these insights because I am convinced that I am essentially seen as worthwhile. In the giving and receiving of intimacy the self is shaped and fired, self-esteem is strengthened and graced.

This process is not simple or smooth. The interactions that build the strengths of intimacy involve a balancing act. There is a tension between two huge tasks in adult development, twin poles that are equally basic and primary to wholeness, the tasks of autonomy and relatedness. We all need to develop independence *and* connectedness. Every human person needs both. One of Carol Gilligan's great insights is that men usually develop autonomy first while women generally develop relatedness first.[3] We all need both.

A tension exists in intimate relationships. How can I give myself appropriately without losing myself? How can I merge with the other and still hold on to a strong sense of my separate self?

The tension often surfaces as fear. Rollo May in *Courage to Create* uses Otto Rank's terms "life fear" and "death fear."[4] "Life fear" is fear of being alone, fear of abandonment, fear that if I am left by the other I will somehow cease to be. It is the fear that gets little children into motion when their parent says, "O.K., if you don't get up I'm going to leave you." It is the fear in countless country songs that say "I can't live without you." It is the fear that led Karen Blixon in the film *Out of Africa* to insist on some kind of commitment from her lover, saying, "I must have someone who belongs to me."

The other fear is what Rank called "death fear." That is the fear of *not* being alone, the fear of being smothered, the fear of being trapped, the fear that the other will become an albatross around my neck, the fear of the other becoming what someone called "an involuntary organ transplant." It is the fear that led Blixon's lover in *Out of Africa* to reply, "I can commit myself, but only one day at a time," and to withdraw.

These two fears are related to the poles of autonomy and relatedness, those strengths that are essential for all of us to develop. Intimate relationships involve a dance between the poles. Closeness has ambiguity. Have I let the other in too far? What will they expect from me, claim from me now? Will they reject me when they know me this deeply? Will I want to reject them?

The process of developing intimacy, then, is both complex and pivotal. If it succeeds, it is a source of rich companioning. While I am capable of being independent, it is wonderful to know I am not alone.

I was once with two priests at the end of a long day. One had been working with me, the other had been working in the parish where we were staying. They were old friends. We were in the living room of the rectory, and they took chairs on either side of the unused ornamental fireplace.

"How was your day?" asked the priest who had been working with me.

"It went pretty well," replied the other man. "The staff got together this morning and really put together some creative things for Lent. There was a lot of discussion, some of it ruffled in places, a few near arguments, but mostly it came out well. I felt good about it."

"And then what did you do?" asked the other priest.

It sounds like a very little thing, but I still remember how it struck me. "And then what did you do?" That simple question spoke eloquently to me. It said I am really interested in your day. I care about it all. I have room, not just to hear the headlines, or hear the first incident, but I want to know anything at all that you want to tell me. It had such an attentiveness to its tone, such a receptivity, that it conveyed a history of having walked together a long, loving journey. It has stayed with me like a refrain: "And then what did you do?"

Intimacy is deep, mutual, trusting, loyal, vulnerable love. It is love that confronts when blind spots surface, love that honors the separateness *and* the bond. It is here that I discover myself as "I," the other as "Thou." It is the place, as we heard the Velveteen Rabbit say long ago, where I become Real.

This experience is especially important for priests. Because the priesthood can so easily be a solitary life, because early formation often warned against friendships as a danger, it is very possible for priests to escape intimacy. The priest is a particularly high profile person, especially in his clerical role, and many people relate to priests only in the role and not to the unique and individual persons underneath.

A beautiful book, *A Green Journey* by Jon Hassler, describes the difficulty in this. An Irish parish priest is talking to a visiting bishop from the United States at the end of a long day. He is trying to explain what it is like to be a priest in his village.

> "I have the respect of nearly everyone in Ballybegs. I go into O'Donovan's pub and all the men lift their caps and mumble something subservient to me as I pass along the bar. There is even one old man who genuflects, I swear to God. Out on the street—you saw it yourself if you came through the town—the priest gets nothing but worshipful smiles and esteem."
>
> "Yes, that's how I see it."
>
> "I'm 66, Bishop. Since the day of my ordination I've been that sort of prince. Now, your average Irish priest, it's to his liking, it's grand with him, being a prince. It makes him strut, if you catch my meaning, and I'm not saying he's a bad priest because of it. I'm only saying I'm not your average Irish priest. I've lived a lifetime as a prince and I'm not finding it a pleasant thing to look back on. It's kept me separate from my people, it has, my eminence has. Prevented me from being close to anyone. . . . I'm standing up there at Christmas saying I love my people, and I'm wishing I had a friend among them. . . . I'm held in esteem by them all, but what's esteem worth in the end? Esteem is fine for the likes of Johnnie Horgan and bruiser O'Connor and Mick the Runt—talk to them for two minutes and you see they're grand boys for esteem—but I'd exchange all the esteem in the world for a single friend."[5]

The building of friendship, the growing strength for loving that comes of being and having friends, is very important for priests. These relationships can take many forms.

There is great richness in friendships with other priests: a bond, a camaraderie, an understanding of two persons who share the same call, the same life-style, the same types of tasks and turmoils and triumphs.

I have been tremendously moved by friendships like this. I remember one in which one of the priests had terribly difficult surgery and later said he could not remember waking up a single time that his friend was not there sitting with him. I remember another in which the two men went on vacation together every year. They would rest and swim and golf and read, but also open their lives in great vulnerability to the scrutiny of the other. There was another old friendship in which one man did an addiction intervention for the other, sticking with him through the whole agonizing recovery process, celebrating with him each year of sobriety. There was another instance where I observed two priests with a deep bond. Each preached at his friend's mother's funeral. In each case the son would try to do the homily himself. In each case he got to a point where he could not go on. He stepped down and his friend took over, completing the words on the Scripture and her life.

There can be great intimacy between priests. There can also be important camaraderie between priests and other men. Significant relationships grow up between boyhood friends or men in the parish or someone met on a tennis court or a picket line.

There can also be tremendous growth and life in deep friendships with women. In former years this was looked upon with strong negative judgment. If a priest was talking to a woman in a rectory, the parlor door had to be left open. In some dioceses a priest's own mother could not ride in the front seat of his car with him lest someone take scandal.

Despite this attitude, there is a long tradition of powerful celibate relationships between priests and women in our Church history. The names of towering figures come to mind, like John of the Cross and Teresa of Avila, Jane de Chantal and Francis de Sales, Francis of Assisi and Clare. When these great loves of our heritage are reviewed, some people have remarked that they were not held up as ideals until they were safely dead. There is undoubtedly some truth to that. The normalization of friendships between priests and women is a recent thing.

Some would say that the breaking down of old barriers was a "summer school phenomenon." When there was great need to be updated after Vatican II, priests and sisters went to school together for the first time since grade school. Many no longer wore the habit or clerical garb. Many called each other by their first names. In addition to classes, there were concerts and picnics and plays to attend. As was inevitable for people with no experience in relating to each other in informal peer roles, there were surging adolescent feelings and a great deal of immature behavior. Many even left priesthood or religious life because they thought that they could not integrate their experiences with their ongoing commitment to ministry. It was a very important, though awkward, transition time in the Church. An interchange of real people outside a role was made possible.

Many priests discovered that relating to women as equals, as peers, broke them open in a new way to the reality of who they themselves were. They felt powerfully affirmed and also arrestingly challenged. Some very deep friendships were formed. Their lives were changed.

One priest in a workshop of mine spoke of such a friendship in his life. He was someone admired greatly in the group, and I can still feel the hush that fell as he began. "I have no doubt that I would never be the man I am today without her in my life. She has had more to do with forming me than anyone except my parents. She believed in me but also never let me get away with anything. Through her encouragement and challenge I came up against my false assumptions and my prejudices. I was also drawn to recognize my gifts and tenderness. I owe much to her of who I am able to be as a priest and a man."

Another man, pastor of a very rough inner-city parish in a huge diocese, spoke of a woman friend of his. He told of a day that he had what he considered a breakthrough liturgy with the street kids. It was a moment of reconciliation between two rival gangs. That evening he had an irate phone call from the chancery censoring him for using nonregulation bread for the Eucharist. He hung up in outrage and enormous disheartenment. How could he stay in the priesthood of a Church that missed the point this much?

He pounded on the back door of the convent where his friend lived. She took one look at him and pulled him into the living room. After he spat out the story she said to him, "What you need to do is to sing."

"I can hardly believe it now myself, looking back on it," he said to me. "As I say that to you it sounds utterly schmaltzy. Like something out of *Sound of Music*. But it worked. She called in the other sisters, good women, hardworking and absolutely generous. The heart of our neighborhood. They all had piles of papers to correct, they all had chores in the house. They stood around the piano with us and we sang. We kept going for hours. In between we told every joke we knew. The last song—you are going to think I am making this up, but I swear it really happened—the last song was 'No Man Is an Island.' I went home knowing that was true."

He continued to speak of her. "At that time she was a first grade teacher in our parish school. She taught sixty-five kids to read that year—none of them had been to kindergarten. Now she runs a shelter for homeless women. We have had twenty years of friendship. We gave each other heart and we gave each other hell. She would support me, but also shape me up. I found out I was a person capable of loving."

One reason friendships with women are so important for priests is that there is a basic dynamic as boys grow up that can shut them off from the feminine. Carol Gilligan describes it in *In a Different Voice*. Judith Viorst summarizes it in *Necessary Losses*. The insight stems from the fact that all of us, men and women, were originally merged with our mothers and identified with them. In the first three years, when gender identity is established, the challenge is very different for boys and girls.

> Girls, to be girls, can define themselves without repudiating their first attachment. Boys to be boys emphatically cannot. Indeed, they must develop what psychoanalyst Robert Stoller calls "symbiosis anxiety," a protective shield against their own strong yearning to merge with Mommy, a shield which preserves and extends their maleness.
>
> In their second and third years of life, then, boys will decisively turn away from their mother. They de-identify with what she is. But their pulling away, their protective shield, may involve a number of anti-female defenses. And so it may be that the price males pay for de-identification is a disdain, a contempt, sometimes even a hatred for women, a disowning of the "feminine" parts of themselves, and an enduring fear of intimacy because it undermines the separation upon which their male identity has been founded.[6]

Because seminary and novitiate training often involves a totally male environment, the estrangement from the feminine can be easily reinforced. A priest's beginning to trust and share with women in deep friendship can contribute a great deal to the healing of this early and functional fear. These friendships can lead to an openness that enhances a priest's ability to interact in his ministry.

This train of thought was expanded by a wise and beloved theologian. He was talking to me about celibacy. He said, "I am convinced that we have *got* to have personal, loving relationships. If someone is afraid of loving, they cannot be a celibate. Celibacy only makes sense if a person knows how to love. No one can love in general if they do not love in the particular."

Then, with a twinkle in his eye, he continued, "I tell my seminarians, 'If you've got to choose, choose women. Women can tell men things they need to hear. The friendships are very fruitful.'"

He leaned forward, grinning, and told me something as if in confidence. "When I celebrated my fortieth anniversary of ordination, my homily was on the women in my life. It was a big risk, but I needed to say it. I told them that I had entered the minor seminary at twelve, and all I heard about was that women were a danger. Lo and behold, what I discovered was that women were the biggest grace, the greatest support. The danger I found was from the unscrupulous use of power in an institution that was very scarred. That is what almost drove me from the priesthood. The scandal of the use of power. It was from the encouragement and modeling of women that I gathered the strength to stay."

I found this a very moving revelation. I want, however, to add something. Friendships with women are important for priests. This is especially true because the majority of the people in congregations, the majority of people on professional and volunteer staffs, will be women. It is crucial for any priest to be able to understand and relate comfortably with women. It is also rich and fruitful to have relationships with other men. The concept of homosexual friendship in priestly life, while beyond the scope of this chapter, is an area that deserves full treatment in its own right. On this topic (as well as on the whole area of sexuality and intimacy in the life of priests) I recommend Donald Goergen's excellent book *The Sexual Celibate.*[7]

An important question centers around the issue of romantic attraction. Certainly this is sometimes present in intimate relationships. Attraction and falling in love, both between and among the sexes, is a reality in the life of priests that generates both delight and trepidation. Relationships with romantic attraction have enormous power, an archetypal power that comes from deep in the unconscious. Psychic projections are unleashed that cause us to see the other in the rose-gold light of the ideal. Phrases like "woman of my dreams" and "man for me," "the perfect match" and "the one I have been waiting for," sound out of our depths. There is a sense of having known one another forever, of being totally close. We are up in the air or down in the dumps, depending on how the other is relating to us.

This is a temporary state, one into which, if we see the other person on a regular basis, sooner or later reality will intrude. It is not a state in which anyone should ever make a life decision. It is always at least partly an illusion.

It can, however, be a transforming state. The Greeks would say that we are walking on Mount Olympus in this state. It is a time we see things from a godlike perspective. We have great tolerance for failures and foibles in the beloved. We are almost spontaneously forgiving. We feel one with all of life. It is as if the light of love streams through the stained glass window of existence, and we see the fragments of life as no longer random or jagged but as the perfectly fitted scarlet and cobalt and emerald of the rose window of the cathedral of being. We are touched by all of life: boys sliding in the drenched grass, the smell of the wind and the curve of the moon, trust from a toddler and a grandmother's musings, sky in a puddle and the sound of a piano far away.

When we have intimate relationships with the added power of attraction and wonder, they turn our world around. It is crucial to realize that this does not mean a person must leave the seminary or priesthood. It is an experience that points to God and to union within ourselves at the same time it points to the other person. It is an experience to be claimed and understood and cherished. It is very possible for this experience to mellow and grow into a deeply loving friendship.

This is not simple, but it can be done. It is not easy to manage to avoid exclusivity and genitality, to find ways to connect and not consume, to bond and not possess. But it is possible. At times the cost is very high. It would be important not to underestimate the courage and perseverance, discipline and trust, that is required to forge deep yet open intimacy like this. I have been honored to be a witness, a deeply moved listener, to some of these relationships. I have been touched and changed by the heroic and humorous love.

There seem to be seasons to them, times of enormous struggle and times of heartstopping joy. There are attempts, honestly and generously wrought, to keep faithful to the love and faithful to commitments. The integrity and energy of these relationships have poured forth compassion and dedication into other personal and ministerial relationships.

Often people raise the question, What about the physical? We are so afraid in our tradition of physical expression. We dread sexual involvement as the worst of all sins. Finding appropriate physical expression doesn't happen simply. Like anything worthwhile, it takes effort and learning.

Perhaps the most important tool to have is an attitude of learning. It is important to really talk together about understandings and boundaries and to use them to reflect on how time is spent together. Choosing together what is most life giving is crucial, asking not so much the question, What exactly are we doing? as How are we loving?

Will there be mistakes? Probably. When my youngest child was learning to ride a bike his brother said to him, ''Face it, Boo, there's no way to learn to ride a bike without losing some skin.'' There is no way to learn anything important without mistakes. The alternatives are to still have training wheels when you are forty or, worse, to never ride at all.

A person who never takes a risk is in danger of being what Gerald Vann calls ''an irreproachable vacuum'' or Loughlan Sofield calls ''a consecrated refrigerator.'' The intention behind the avoidance of any risk is to protect the relationship with God. The difficulty can be what was expressed by an eminent moral theologian who teaches in our program when he said, ''All sorts of people because they love no one imagine that they love God.''

In his excellent chapter in Mary Ann Huddleston's book, *Celibate Loving: An Encounter in Three Dimensions*, Patrick Carroll writes: ''Too often the Church, or a community within the Church, has judged and punished those human frailties occurring in the person honestly trying to learn to love, and it has not even noticed those failures of distance, coldness, and aloofness that destroy the Church and Christ's call to union so the world may believe. . . . In every generation of religious life there have been too many crusty bachelors and mean old maids masquerading as celibates, going to their graves without once letting sex rear its head. Too often love was squelched in the process, and they witnessed to nothing but will power.''

Carroll continues: ''I do not want to minimize the risk involved in living such a project. We risk involvement and pain, risk even sin, and separation from our community or priesthood, risk, in myriad ways, the cross. But I would emphasize that the risk involved in any other project is perhaps more grave. For it is the risk to fail to be a Christian, to fail to love at all. As John Courtney Murray pointed out many years ago, in choosing not to love anyone particularly, personally, uniquely, we risk never loving at all, never being alive at all, never letting Jesus be alive in us.''[8]

I think with sadness at the harm that has been done priests by the lack of official understanding of the importance of the support of friendship. It is crucial that the need be acknowledged and that there be a building of supports by the community or diocese, or an allowing of supports that naturally develop. This is especially important in situations, most often of priests in religious communities, where men are frequently uprooted and moved long distances for new assignments. There can be real wrenching in these moves. The difficulty of keeping friendships alive in letters and phone calls, the emotional strain of reinvesting in new relationships, has perhaps not been sufficiently acknowledged. It seems tragic when a community assigns a man to a living situation that will clearly not be supportive and then judges him harshly when he cannot sustain himself in the isolation.

I think of a gifted, endearing young man, ordained about five years, who was transferred from a dynamic, enthusiastic university parish to a very troubled parish a thousand miles away. Of the five men in his community who were stationed there, three were forty years older than he was and two were active alcoholics. His powerful preaching style and easy charm was seen as a threat by them. Not only did the members of his local community not support him but they criticized most of what he did. They pounced upon his friendship with one of the parish volunteers, a woman in her twenties, as a scandal. He eventually left and married her. While leaving to marry can sometimes be a positive move coming from a realization that a man is in the wrong way of life and is being called to the intimacy of marriage and to other forms of ministry, at other times it is, in actuality, an escape from a situation experienced as desperate. Respectful attention to the need for support and friendship can diminish desperation.

The key in the struggle for warm, authentic, honest celibate loving is a relationship with God that is deep and personal and central and merry. Prayer that again and again confirms God's passionate, creating care makes possible the attempts to love without possessing. Carroll and others in Huddleston's collection express that fact well. A superb reflection on this truth is found in chapter 11 of Sandra Schneider's *New Wineskins: Re-imagining Religious Life Today.*[9]

In an article, "Sex, Sexuality, and Religious Formation," chastity is defined as "the virtue or acquired taste, inclination, and skill by which we willingly integrate our sexual desires into our overall life goals. . . . It is not prudishness, fear, and repression oriented to mere abstinence, but a joyful attempt to bring various parts of one's personality into harmony."[10]

For all of us this harmonizing is a life-work. It is often helpful to have someone we can talk to, a spiritual director or counselor or trusted friend or mentor, who can help us sort out the workings of our relationships. Such a person can make it more possible for us to glean the learnings, to listen for the rationalizations or scrupulosities that can endanger this splendid enterprise. They can keep us honest and keep us celebrating.

These intimacies are great gifts. We do not go looking for them. Sometimes they are given to us. There may be times in our lives when we have a companioning that has unexpected beauty and wonder, the grace of tender reciprocity. There may also be times in our lives when we seem to be called into the emptiest of deserts, times when we are asked to meet God in great alone-ing. Through it all, it is most central to realize that the longing that is known in experiences of union and the longing that is known in times of profound loneliness are both rooted in the longing for God.

Ministry

In the first section of this reflection we have been considering the importance of intimacy in the personal development of a priest. In the second section we will consider the question of the importance of intimacy for the ministry of a priest. Certainly these aspects are not separable; the quality of ministry is directly related to the quality of personal development in a person. But it would be helpful to look at a few points particularly from the perspective of ministry.

Erikson's first three stages of adult development are identity, intimacy and generativity. The strengths of each stage are called upon in the stage that follows. If I have not developed my identity, if I do not have some sense of who I am, then I will have difficulty with intimacy. I have to know myself in order to give myself with some consistency. I need some sense of my boundaries to keep from being taken over by the other person. I need to have some flexibility in my identity to be able to respond and grow in the face of the challenges that intimacy brings. Intimacy tests and strengthens identity.

The third stage of adult development, generativity, calls out my capacity to give myself, to nurture and create new life outside myself. The strengths of this stage empower me to be a parent, to become a mentor, to offer myself in ministry. It is here that I give myself to the larger world that will go on after me, to the next generation, to society, to the people of God.

At this stage, the gift of myself is not essentially reciprocal. I give, not expecting in return. I pour myself out for life. While mutuality is the hallmark of intimacy, it is not necessarily a characteristic of generativity. Parents, teachers, mentors, try to raise children and students to be independent, to lead separate, wholesome lives on their own.

An essential part of the call of a priest is a call to serve, to be a washer of feet. It is a response to the plea of Jesus: "Simon Peter, do you love me? Feed my lambs."

In order to do this for a lifework, strengths built in identity and intimacy stages are crucial. Most people in ministry are underappreciated. There are moments of being highly criticized, or at least taken for granted. If priests do not have sources of intimacy in their lives, they can be in various kinds of danger. One is the likelihood of burning out. They can only go on giving and giving for so long. Their responsibilities get more and more complex, especially as the priest shortage increases. Eventually they may find themselves exhausted and empty. They need a place to go where they can just be themselves, where they are welcomed not for what they do but just for who they are, a place where they can put their feet up and tell the truth and hear the truth about themselves.

Having such a place is important because another danger is that without feedback from people who know them well and love them, priests can operate under distorted images of themselves. They can see themselves as "princes," as "grand boys for esteem," as the character in *A Green Journey* said, or they may see themselves as worthless, as failures, as obsolete and ridiculous. It is their intimate friends who can either challenge their grandiosity or remind them of their greatness.

If priests have no intimacy in their lives they may find themselves meeting their intimacy needs through their ministry. They may have inappropriate physical contact with someone they counsel, they may develop crushes on people they direct. The need for human closeness is fierce, especially in a life where the resources of time and energy are emptied day after day. The hunger will surface.

If there are sources of intimacy with peers, if there are relationships with real mutuality and regular interaction, there is much less likelihood of meeting those needs inappropriately with people being served. The time and energy to develop and nurture deep friendships need to be given priority in the lives of priests. It should be put on their calendars and guarded as sacred. It *is* sacred.

For priests who do not have intimate relationships in their lives, there is a danger beyond that of meeting intimacy needs with those for whom they are responsible. It is possible that they are actually finding their identity under the guise of generativity. Their identity may not have been strengthened and tested in the interchanges of intimacy, and they may find themselves totally identifying with the role. They may function almost as a kind of stereotype. They may find it impossible to share power in ministry because their self-understanding is entirely dependent on it.

A final point about priests and ministry is related to the fact that the work of most priests is to be present at key times in the lives of the people of the Church. A priest presides over moments of worship and is sought out in moments of worry. He baptizes into new life and anoints as life comes to its close. He breaks open the word in the homily and breaks the bread in the Eucharist. He marries and buries and instructs and forgives. He is called to be an interpreter and a companion of this whole journey, which is a lifetime struggle to love. If he himself has never really loved, if he has never really allowed himself to be vulnerable, if he has not experienced intimacy, it is very difficult for him to lead others on this journey. It is almost impossible for him to speak with either compassion or authenticity about what it is like to be human. It is essential for him to know what it is like to need to ask for forgiveness from another person, to have some experience of the humbling, harrowing efforts to communicate that thread through the daily lives of most people. He needs to know both the warmth of closeness and the hard work of relating. He needs to understand that generosity and genuineness are not easily born, that sacrifice and self-gift come with pain. It is important that he know the letting downs and letting gos, the breakdowns and breakthroughs, that can give a merciful sense of real life to his preaching and service.

A priest once spoke to me on a darkening afternoon after one of my workshops. He told me that he had never had a friend. He had kept all the rules through the years, he had done exactly as he was told. "I've never been close to anyone," he said. "I have never really let myself be known. More and more I wonder if I really believe in God. I don't know if God exists or not."

I could feel a lump in my throat. There was such sadness in this hesitant revelation. It was tragic. We spoke for a long time about finding someone to help him sort all this through.

I also felt the tragedy for the people in his parish. What happens for the people when a person like this is their priest? How could he possibly mediate meaning in the lives of people who were straining and daring and grappling with life, trying beyond all odds to go on loving? When relationship *is* the message, how can it be conveyed by someone who does not know how to relate? It does not happen in words. It happens in love.

Noninvolvement is one style of a priest who cannot relate. Another is the style of aggression. I remember years ago another priest I had seen over a period of years. Almost every Sunday he had some kind of blowup. He spewed forth his outrage on the altar boys or lectors or Eucharistic ministers. That he had been the priest, the only priest, for the people in that parish for ten years was frightening. I think he, too, had never had a friend.

144 Patricia H. Livingston

Spirituality

The final area of our reflection is the importance of intimacy for the spirituality of the priest. Certainly spirituality is not separate from personal development or from ministry; we are only choosing to look at it individually.

An insight provided by the writings of theologian Rosemary Haughton is that God *is* relationship. God *is* exchange of life, Father to Son through Spirit. There is no moment of stillness, it is a constant outpouring, a giving and receiving that is endless and total.

When we love, when we engage in the giving and receiving that define intimacy, we are doing what God *is*. It is as sacred as that.

Historical theologian Michael Himes speaks of God not as being a lover, but as being *Love*, God as the relationship between the three persons. The word "God," he says, is the name of the relationship. When we enter into intimacy, we experience the essence of God.

Himes describes the great commandments in the Gospels. In Mark, the scribe says to Jesus that the first commandment is to love God and the second is identical, to love your neighbor as yourself. This scribe is the only person who is praised by Jesus in all of Mark. Jesus says of him, "You are very close to the kingdom." The truth Himes extols is that Jesus has equated what we have thought of as two separate commandments. In the Gospel of John they are given as one: "I leave you one new commandment, love one another as I have loved you." When you love one another, you are loving me. When you feed the hungry, visit the imprisoned, clothe the naked, you do not do it *for* me, you do it *to* me.[11]

Human love is mysteriously interwoven with God's love. It also illuminates God's love. If we have never been well loved, it will be difficult to ever grasp the reality of God's love. The priest on the dark afternoon went through the motions that corresponded to the words for thirty years of priesthood, but from the wasteland of his childhood and the barren stretch of his adulthood there was nothing that opened the reality of God's presence for him. "Does God exist or not? I do not know."

In the breathtaking experience of the uniqueness of another human person in their multicolored, laughing, aching freshness, we find ourselves knowing ever more deeply that God is More. The contours of God expand and enrich. We genuflect before the mystery.

Recently in our institute we were faithsharing in pairs about Matthew's account of the transfiguration. I was seated with a priest from the Southwest, a powerful, practical, angular man, a leader in his diocese and beloved member of our group. As we pored over the passage together, we were both very moved by the way Jesus approached the disciples when they had thrown themselves to the ground after hearing the voice of the Father speak to Jesus from the cloud filled with great light. We agreed that our summary of it would be God touches us in our fear. We talked about experiences of fear. I was thinking of the fear that is dread, of terror, of the inbreaking of some kind of terrible impending loss and pain. I was speaking out of recent experiences of this kind of fear, and of the utter tenderness of God's touch in that time. My companion listened to me with an attention I can only describe as reverent.

Then he spoke of the kind of fear he had in mind. "I was thinking more of the fear of awe," he said, "the absolute awe at the beauty in the heart of another person I have been allowed to love." It was amazing to hear him speak in this kind of poetic language. He was dressed in jeans and boots and a simple country shirt. "It is as if the door to the sanctuary within them has opened, and the light of the holy floods out. I know in that moment, almost as if God has spoken it, that they are God's beloved one. I feel the fear that is awe, and I understand why the disciples fell to the ground at the transfiguration. In that fear God touches me, as Jesus touched them, and says, 'Do not be afraid.' I have always loved the part where the Gospel says, 'When they looked around they saw only Jesus.' When I am moved to awe at the holy, the beauty, in the other person who has let me know them, let me love them, I know that in some way I am seeing Jesus. It is *only* my friend, as it was for the disciples *only* Jesus. It is Jesus. It is the beloved one.''

Our experience of love, our knowledge of relationship, reveals God's love to us. At the same time, our relationship with God clarifies and transforms our experiences of relationship with others. They are intertwined. The deepest part of the mystery is somehow contained here. Human love leads us to God's love without for a moment taking away from the endearing uniqueness of that love itself. It is not disembodied or abstracted as it reveals God. Somehow it becomes even more deeply human and real. At the same time, God's presence in the love extends and expands it in a way that is very necessary for the survival of the love. A great temptation, especially in times of full intensity of feeling, is to imagine that in this loving bond we will somehow meet all of each other's needs, that we will totally fulfill each other. This is impossible, and the expectation, whether spoken or unspoken, can weigh down a relationship and eventually destroy it. No other person can ever fill what Sebastian Moore calls our ''ineluctable longing.''[12] That yearning will always be at the heart of us. It is the great energy of desire at the center of the human condition. It is what propels us into the search for the Perfect Match and the search for the Holy Grail. It is Augustine's restlessness for the Beauty, ever ancient, ever new. It is vital to understand our reaching for the other as part of that holiest of hungers.

Intimacy and the Life of a Priest

Intimacy has an axial role in a priest's development, in his ministry, in his relationship with God. Unfortunately, intimacy is often not only not supported but is actively discouraged. Negative voices are heard not only externally from traditional formation and well-meaning critics but also in the form of internal messages of distrust and dualism. Perhaps it is in hearing the stories that we most come to trust. A final story:

He had served most of his priesthood in the mission territory of a primitive, tropical country. His fair Irish skin had been burned again and again until there was a network of lines around his eyes and his mouth. He looked tired, worn beyond his years, but filled with peace.

It was high summer after an especially endless winter when he told me his story. We were walking, unconsciously adjusting our stride to each other, mile after mile in a late afternoon. He wanted me to know about his great love, a woman he had met during his sabbatical home from the missions. They had been on a team together doing a project.

"It was a whole new experience to let myself be loved," he said with a shyness, looking away from me, but wanting to go on. "I had to learn to receive. I had spent my ministerial life thinking that the whole point of our call was the giving, that we were meant to always be pouring out. I operated out of a desire to serve, but there came with that a kind of detachment. I had deep faith, but somehow I couldn't really feel with the people.

"When Sarah and I met after class or after a work session, she began to listen to me, inviting me to talk about myself. It was almost foreign to me. I was amazed by her response. As I found myself faltering along, trying to put things into words that I had never said out loud, she was touched." He stammered a little here, seeming to find it almost hard to speak. But he went on. "It was as if she saw a goodness in me, simple as I am. I could see that goodness reflected in her face. Then I had to tell her about the ways I am not good. About the times I have let people down. About the times I have caused people pain. She listened to all of that too. And then an amazing thing happened. I found myself telling her about my own hurts. About anguish I knew I had, and then other anguish that I had not even known I had. It was as if, here with her, it was at last safe to feel the pain. To recognize and name the wounds. In her unspeakable tenderness I was able to express them, to honor them, to hold them up to forgiveness and to love.

"It transformed my image of God. I began for the first time to have a sense of what God's faithfulness is. My brokenness was reverenced and held. I saw myself as flawed and weak and sinful, but in all of it immeasurably loved. *Loved.* And even found beautiful." His voice was very soft when he said the last phrase as if he still found that very hard to believe.

"I also learned that what I give to God matters greatly. I didn't realize I didn't know that. I was not conscious that my sense of God was almost remote, as if God did not really need anything from me. I know now that God has a vulnerability and an eagerness for love. I know that because it was so profound in my experience of her. It mattered to her when I listened. It *changed* her that I found her lovely. Because that realization was so profound, I now am sure there is no such thing as a divine indifference."

We walked for a while, the shadows of the trees lengthening, the breeze picking up around the lake. At last I said, "And then what did you do?"

"I went back to the missions when the program was over. I missed her dreadfully. And yet my love for her continued to grow. And in some way that is hard to explain. I was released to love where I was. It was as if I had been opened up, broken open, really. I had access to a texture of life I could not feel before. As I experienced the lives of my people, I came to the place of their dire pain with a mute and stark empathy. I sensed the simplest joys as utter generosity. I had much more patience with the dark, much more wonder at the light.

"I was changed with the people. I felt like a brother to them more than a minister. One day they were having a festival, and they called out to me to join the dancing. I am very self-conscious about my own awkwardness, and I had always refused their entreaties before. Something came over me, and I found myself moving into the circle. I did not do it out of duty, out of some idea that they would feel as if I were interested in them if I did. It was not to honor them. I did it for myself, as if I might somehow be one with them in my own soul, that I might be lightened and freed in the dancing, that I might express in my body the oneness of the human condition. I must have looked off balance and unsure, because one of the smallest children in the village took me by the hand: 'I will show you, stay with me.' "

He paused here, caught deep in the memory. His voice was husky and his eyes began to fill as he continued, "I did it. I danced. I joined in the dance. With the background of their high pitched pipes and strong drums I moved with them between the earth and the sky. Dancing. Dancing love. Dancing God."

He and I walked a long time after that, walked into the last of the sun and the beginning of the night. We did not speak again.

It reminded me of another afternoon a thousand miles away on the far coast of the continent when I stood in the sand by a monk with a blue watch who knelt and wept.

God breaks in with love.

Notes

1. Erik H. Erikson, *Childhood and Society*, 2nd ed. (New York: Norton, 1963) 263.

2. Evelyn Eaton and James D. Whitehead, *Christian Life Patterns* (New York: Doubleday, 1979) 73.

3. See esp. Gilligan's treatment of this, *In a Different Voice: Psychological Theory and Women's Development* (Cambridge, Mass.: Harvard University Press, 1982).

4. Rollo May, *Courage to Create* (New York: Norton, 1975) 11.

5. Jon Hassler, *A Green Journey* (New York: Ballantine Books, 1985) 218–219.

6. Judith Viorst, *Necessary Losses* (New York: Ballantine Books, 1986) 121–122.

7. Donald Goergen, *The Sexual Celibate* (New York: Doubleday, 1979).

8. L. Patrick Carroll, "Becoming a Celibate Lover," *Celibate Loving: Encounter in Three Dimensions*, ed. Mary Ann Huddleston, (New York: Paulist, 1984) 116–117.

9. Sandra Schneiders, *New Wineskins: Re-imagining Religious Life Today* (New York: Paulist, 1986) ch. 11.

10. Anonymous, "Sex, Sexuality, and Religious Formation," *The CMI Journal*, vol. 2 (1988) 9–10. (Communication Ministry, Inc.)

11. These reflections by Michael Himes are drawn from his lectures at the Center for Continuing Formation in Ministry, University of Notre Dame, 1990.

12. Sebastian Moore, *The Inner Loneliness* (New York: Crossroad, 1982).

The Priesthood and Celibacy

Matthew H. Clark, D.D.

Donald Goergen's invitation to contribute a chapter on priestly celibacy to this volume came as quite a surprise. I was flattered that he would think of me as a pastor in the Church who would have something of value to say on the subject. I also felt deeply challenged by his invitation to offer public pastoral comments about a theme which has a high and controversial profile in the Church in the United States and which is of strong concern to so many persons. I count myself among those who are concerned, and I have tried to share those concerns with some brother bishops, with many of our priests, and with various groups of men and women religious and laypersons in our own diocese and in several others I have been privileged to visit.

Talk of mandatory celibacy for diocesan priests is very much a part of daily life. It has been for a number of years, but questions about its meaning, its value relative to other values in the Church, and its effects in the lives of people come more and more to the fore, at least in my own personal experience as a bishop.

In our own diocese we are, through our Commitment to Ministry program, asking parish communities to face what we anticipate will be a rapid decline in the number of priests we will have available for service over the next ten years. Our people have responded to that invitation with a spirit of faith and generosity that I have found quite remarkable. They are creative in developing ways of cooperation that will free our priests to serve in two or more communities, each of which not long ago was accustomed to having its own resident pastor. These parish communities are the more energetic and creative in their response when we place problems before them and enlist their help in solving them.

But generous as they are, the people of our diocese are asking questions that are challenging because their questions relate to the centrality of the Eucharist in Catholic life, the relationship of the ministerial priesthood to the Eucharist, and the relationship of celibacy to the priesthood. What emerges from these faithful people more and more frequently is wonder that we seem to place in jeopardy the accustomed frequent celebration of the Eucharistic liturgy, which has been at the core of our Catholic life, in order to uphold the value of mandatory celibacy, which is acknowledged universally to be not essential to the priesthood. It is not that people are arguing that celibacy is not worthwhile, or that it is not fitting that the priest should be celibate, or that celibacy is not a cherished gift from God, or that it is not a revered tradition in the Church. Rather, what they are saying in a nutshell is that if we really believe what we say about the Eucharist, then we had better take a long, careful look at the value we place on mandatory priestly celibacy and assess the price we are willing to pay to preserve it in the Latin Church.

We recently experienced a similar kind of reaction in a related venture. We have made a special effort on a diocesan-wide basis to invite our people to identify and forward to us the names of young men in their parish communities in whom they see qualities that suit them for priesthood. The response to our Call to Priesthood program has been gratifying. Parish priests carefully introduced the program over a period of several weeks; our communities offered prayers for God's blessings on the program. Then some seven hundred names were submitted, and we sent personal invitations to all of them to attend a day designed to provide them with both information about ordained priesthood that would be helpful to them and the opportunity to meet like-minded young men.

Some eighty young men turned out for that day and a second one like it. They were quite positive about the experience. A strong feature of the day was the opportunity it offered them to be in the company of so many other men who were going through a period of search and questioning similar to their own. Another strong common note was their concern about committing themselves to a life of celibate chastity. The language the men used varied, of course, but it interested me very much that their concern centered around the loneliness and lack of support they perceived to be inescapably part of the celibate priest's life-style.

Interesting to me as that day and the comments of the young men were, there were no great surprises in it. It is very much the common experience of vocation people today to encounter concerns, fears, and worries about celibacy so strong as to discourage the young men who express them from testing out what otherwise seem like vocations to the priesthood. I think that this experience is not merely personal or anecdotal. Studies seem to support rather strongly what I hear in conversations with people from all parts of the country. Mandatory priestly celibacy is a major barrier to young men who would be attracted to the ordained priesthood if that obligation did not exist.

Even in the letters of recommendation to our Call to Priesthood program which we received from all over the diocese, mention was frequently made of the celibacy requirement. "I am sending this name even though I am sure John wants to marry." "I would have sent Sam's name in but I know he would never want to be celibate all of his life." And some correspondents who sent in names took considerable pains to express displeasure that the Church would insist on this discipline of mandatory, lifelong celibacy when, by all available evidence, that insistence seems to block a large number of otherwise attractive vocational possibilities.

These two specific experiences of our diocese are neither atypical nor isolated. Rarely does more than a day or two go by that the subject of priesthood or ministry or vocation does not come up in my life and work as a bishop. And such conversations seldom proceed for more than five minutes without someone's raising the issue of mandatory celibacy and, in a great majority of instances, raising the question as to why we are so insistent on its preservation.

I think it is important to stress here that I am not referring just to a particular segment of our Catholic population. I am not reporting on views of just the young or the college educated, or the single or the married, or clergy or laity. I am talking about a broad cross section of our population: faithful, good people who love the Church, who are loyal to it, but who raise the question: Why require celibacy? What good does it do if it keeps people from the priesthood? And, as I indicated earlier, I believe that the experience I have is not notably different from that of other bishops in other parts of our country. The issue is alive and is the subject of much discussion in the local Churches.

I have tried to listen carefully to the people as they have raised their concerns and questions and expressed their visions and dreams about priesthood and celibacy. A bishop cannot ignore them, I think, and be faithful to his call to be in touch with the faith and wisdom of the people of God. My listening tells me that we, the whole Church, need somehow to attend to this matter in fresh and creative ways.

Exactly how this might best be done I do not know, but I would suggest, at least, that some aspects of mandatory celibacy and its implications for the Church need to be dealt with if we ever hope to recover a deeper regard for priestly life and to attract worthy candidates to the ministerial priesthood.

We need to find better ways to hear and learn from the experience of the people of the Church in the areas of sexuality, marriage, birthing, and parenting. In my opinion our

Catholic heritage is rich and strong in what it says about these themes and about the dignity of the human person in general. But I do believe that, in our age, the credibility of the Church and of ordained churchmen is often not high when we address issues of sexuality. We are often seen as unaware of or unaffected by the day-to-day experiences of faithful Catholic people.

This perceived lack of credibility carries over to the issue of celibacy. If fairly large numbers of people find the Church not strongly credible in matters of sexuality, it follows that they may not place a great deal of trust in what we have to say about celibacy.

In addition to listening to the people, we need to be open to the experience of priests as they reflect on priestly celibacy. For example, in my home diocese of Albany, large numbers of ordained priests have left the active ministry since 1960. In my experience as director of Albany's Priests' Personnel Board between November 1969 and June 1972, I must have interviewed at least twenty priests who were leaving the priesthood. There have been many more since then. The Diocese of Rochester has had a similar experience. A large number of the priests of our diocese have resigned from the active ministry in the last thirty years. And, although the annual number of priests resigning has diminished in recent years, the rate of attrition is still higher than anyone likes. To illustrate that, I mention that in the eleven years I have been the bishop of Rochester, I have ordained thirty-five priests for the service of our diocese. Of that number, five have resigned from the active ministry.

These have been and are painful realities for the two dioceses I have mentioned. When a priest who has made such a personal investment of himself for the service of the community judges that it is necessary to pull up roots and start on a new path in life, it is difficult both for him and for the community because of the bonds of respect and affection that have developed between them. It is obviously a doubly troubled circumstance when neither the priest nor the community can understand well why, ordinarily, in the Latin Rite of the Roman Catholic Church marriage and priestly identity and vocation are judged to be incompatible, whereas they are not so judged in some other rites or in other Christian Churches.

Once again, the great majority of the priests to whom I have just referred would choose to remain in active priestly ministry were they able to do that as married men. And it is my understanding that at least a solid majority of our own active diocesan priests would be very much open to that possibility.

It is true that not all of those individuals who have resigned would have stayed if they could have married. Some were quite frank in saying that they knew well that they should never have been ordained in the first place. There were a variety of reasons for that, but whatever the reason, they knew with certainty that they had set out on the wrong path to begin with.

Besides the personal pain that inevitably attaches to such decisions, for all concerned, I think there is another implication to be dealt with. It is the effect that the reality of so many departures of good, holy priests from active ministry has on potential candidates for the priesthood. If our brothers have been saying that, notwithstanding their honest efforts, they were not able to sustain a life of celibacy and still live a life that left them in reasonable peace and happiness, this fact has a powerful impact on our young men.

The message they derive from these departures, incorrectly I think, is that the lives of priests are, in general, characterized by loneliness and isolation. When this is coupled, as it so often is, with a societal, cultural message that says one cannot be happy apart from a sexually active life, it is understandable why some young men have second thoughts about entering the seminary. And it is understandable when similar attitudes are present in the minds of their parents.

At least such considerations as these are how I am best able to make sense out of the small number of young men we are able to attract to the priesthood. I say that because studies indicate the strongest influences in attracting young men to the priesthood are family influence and the example of priests who live fruitful, happy lives. In the two dioceses in the United States in which I have been privileged to serve as a priest, there are good numbers both of families who encourage their sons to consider vocations to the priesthood and of priests who are eminently effective and beloved pastoral ministers. Consequently, I am puzzled why the clear, good example of those families and those priests is not more effective in encouraging our young men to consider priesthood.

Other good people see the issue differently. They say that we have lost our focus, that the Church has in recent years abandoned the kinds of discipline and order that once attracted solid young men to the priesthood. Further, they read recent phenomena like the emergence of the laity, the restoration of the permanent diaconate, and the rapid development of a variety of lay ministries as having the effect of weakening the position of the ordained priest in the community. Their perception is that the identity and mission of the priest have been blurred in all of this and that we will not enjoy an increased number of candidates for the ordained priesthood unless we deal with those issues.

This is a view shared by a fair number of our priests, although by far fewer than a majority of them. Some ask, "What's left for us to do?" and in the asking summarize and express what their like-minded colleagues are thinking and feeling. Their morale is weakened by what they experience as a double bind: a loss of authority coupled with ever-increasing calls to relate to other persons in the Church as responsible co-workers and collaborators in making decisions once reserved to the ordained priest. It is interesting to me that priests of this disposition tend to attract potential candidates for the seminary in slightly larger numbers than others, but that these young men tend to yearn for ordained ministry of the type we experienced in the preconciliar Church.

My concern for these young men is that the Church no longer trains its seminarians for that kind of priesthood. Rather the Church orders its programs of priestly formation to train ordained ministers to serve in a Church whose self-awareness is not exactly the same as it was before Vatican Council II.

* * * * *

July 15, 1962, was a hot day in Rome. I remember the day well because it was my twenty-fifth birthday and it was the day on which six of my classmates at the North American College were to be ordained priests and the other sixty-two of us were to be ordained subdeacons. In those years one's ordination to the subdiaconate was the occasion when one made a public, solemn commitment to a life of celibate chastity and to the daily praying of the Liturgy of the Hours.

As I remember that day, twenty-eight years later, I am filled with fond memories of associations with schoolmates and mentors, many of which have blossomed into lifelong friendships. We were, if I may say so, good young men and those charged with responsibility for our formation were persons of high quality. All of us seminarians were quite serious about the work of preparing for priesthood and I think it's fair to say that if all of us didn't give 100 percent effort all of the time, we came quite close to that.

In the years since that day in 1962, three members of our class have died. Of those still living, 50 percent have resigned from the active priestly ministry. I have not taken a poll of those good friends, but informal, sometimes indirect contacts with them and my general experience since then lead me to believe that 95 percent of them left the active ministry primarily because they wished to marry. And the great majority of them, I believe, would gladly have continued to serve the Church as ordained ministers had they been allowed to do that as married men.

What happened between all of the hard work and years of preparation by those young men in the late fifties and early sixties and their departure from the active ministry, which began not long after our ordination and which continues even to this day? Was there something completely wrong with our program of formation as it was structured in those days? Was it a sound program that was mishandled by those charged with its administration? Were those who later resigned somehow dishonest when they made their commitments? Or were they uninformed as to what the obligation to celibacy would mean as their lives unfolded? Or were they unwilling or unable to pay the price that a life of celibacy sometimes carries with it? And why are one-half of our number still engaged in active priestly ministry? Were we the more informed or honest or generous or realistic half of the group? Were we more sensitive to and courageous in responding to God's call in our lives?

And what about the quality of priestly service of those of us who remain active in ordained priestly ministry? Are we truly loving people who somehow attract others to and remind them of the love of Christ? If we are, is that precious capacity enhanced by our celibate life-style? If we are not the kind of loving people we want to be, would we be any different if we were free to marry? And if we were married, would that reality diminish our capacity lovingly to serve among the people as ordained priests?

These are some of the questions that come to my mind as I remember that day in July of 1962 and those dear, gifted men with whom I celebrated our ordinations. There may be many other, more significant questions to be raised. But I do know that these questions are real for me and that questions like them are much discussed and puzzled over in the Church.

One response to the realities implied in these questions is the change that has taken place in programs of priestly formation in the years since Vatican Council II. In our day the program was mediated by a rather detailed rule and supporting daily schedule. A seminarian's life was ordered in fine detail. Indeed it was ordered in such detail that a student could be located at any moment of the day or night save for those afternoons when he was permitted to take walks in the city. We all rose at 5:30 A.M., and the lights in all rooms were extinguished by a central switch at 10:00 P.M.

The fine priests who were generous enough to serve as our formation staff were charged with seeing to it that we understood and observed that rule. I know that they cared about us students, but they were discouraged from developing personal relationships with us. Even if the style of the day had fostered that kind of relationship, it would have been quite difficult for them. We were some two hundred and fifty students; they were only six in number and had multiple collateral duties. In the more specific ministry of spiritual direction, there were two priests assigned to deal with that large number of students. Those numbers meant that however generous those two men were, personal interviews with students could not be frequent or regular. One practical effect of that ratio was that stress was placed on conferences on spiritual matters given to the whole community by one of the spiritual directors or by a guest retreat director rather than on individual consultations.

In an environment like that, I did not find a strong invitation or opportunity to discuss much that was deeply personal to me, including my own sexuality and the human implications of the life of celibacy to which I was about to commit myself.

Our program of formation, as I have said, was mediated by rules, not by relationships. A saying popular at the time indicated that if you kept the rule, the rule would keep you. Discipline, duty, and sacrifice were familiar words in that environment. Discovery, deepening, and growth were not.

All of my relationships in those four years just prior to my ordination were with the men with whom I lived. We were two hundred and fifty males living in a seminary, attending a virtually all-male university, and living a schedule that made relationships outside of those circles close to impossible.

It is my opinion that while many good things happened during those years, there were other facets of our life that were not constructive. I believe that the isolation of those years did little to contribute to our maturity. I would say the same about the almost total lack of interaction with women and about the very restricted range of choices open to us in daily living. It seems paradoxical that we were expected to make decisions in those years that would last for a lifetime and touch the very core of our being in an environment in which someone else decided when we were ready for sleep and how much rest we needed. And it strikes me as no less paradoxical that we were preparing to engage with other people, indeed to lead them, in many of life's most deeply significant moments by being almost totally apart from them for four years. And all of this when we were in our early twenties.

Much of that has since changed. When I had the privilege of returning to that same seminary as spiritual director in 1973, we operated under the Program for Priestly Formation newly developed by the National Conference of Catholic Bishops (NCCB) and approved by the Vatican's Congregation for Catholic Education. That program placed much more emphasis on growth through relationships and reflection on life experience than through the observance of a detailed rule and daily schedule. It placed great stress on interaction between the student and his faculty advisor and spiritual director. It also incorporated into the program of formation some experience of ministry. In addition, the seminary environment was a more open one. Guests were welcome in our house, and students were much freer than in my day to determine how and when they would focus their energies. They were expected to be faithful to academic and spiritual requirements and to be active participants in community life. But they enjoyed much more opportunity to make decisions and to be accountable for them than we had. When students complained that they should have more freedom, one or another of us "old-timers" would post the daily schedule from our seminary years on the bulletin board. That schedule always evoked much laughter among the students and, for a time at least, modified their concerns about the demands we placed on them.

My memory of those days in the seventies is that the more expansive environment called for by the renewed program of priestly formation was itself a help in preparing the students for a commitment to celibacy. The expectation was that each student would be in frequent and regular contact with an advisor and a spiritual director to whom he would be accountable for the way he was responding to the program of formation to which the Church was calling him. And the student could expect that the faculty member would offer whatever guidance and support he could to help the student to discern his vocation and to pursue it with self-knowledge and generosity.

The genuine attempt made to create a healthy environment did not guarantee perfect results. But it was my experience that all of us, faculty and students, tried, just as the earlier generation had tried, to be faithful to what was asked of us. The students of those days communicated more frequently and, I am quite sure, much more deeply with us faculty members than we communicated with our faculty when we were students. This is not a comment about the talent or virtue of the people in either generation. It is rather a comment on shifts in the way the Church understood it and put that self-understanding into practice in very concrete ways in the program of priestly formation.

Today another shift in the Church's self-understanding is occurring among our people, supported by the theological emphases of Vatican Council II and by enriched insight into the sacramental significance of baptism and matrimony. There is now a growing recognition that Christian marriage, with the intimate sexual relations it blesses, is not inferior to Christian celibacy as a way of responding to the gospel but is, like such celibacy, an extension of one's personal vocation founded in baptism. Implicit in this evolving recognition is a reasonable questioning not of celibacy in itself but of its mandatory status in relation to ordained priesthood.

A further consequence of this development is that today the very mandatoriness of celibacy as a requirement for priestly ordination ends up deflecting emphasis and value from both priesthood and celibacy. This is an unintended but nonetheless logical outcome of the Church's just appreciation of Christian marriage, and both priesthood and celibacy freely chosen for the sake of the gospel suffer.

In other eras of the Church, this unwitting deflection of ecclesial priority from the cherished ministry of ordained priesthood itself and from the cherished witness of celibacy itself to the mandatory linking of the two may not have occurred, but it has strikingly occurred today for reasons I have reflected on earlier in this essay. In the collective mind of Catholic people today, so much attention is given to mandatory celibacy in relation to ordained priesthood that attention is to a considerable extent inevitably shifted away from the Church's great need to celebrate and call forth the ministry of ordained priesthood and to encourage and welcome the public witness of celibacy for the sake of the reign of God. By making a required connection between these two charisms such a priority, we in effect undervalue both of these precious gifts in the Christian community. Despite the centuries of this law, the Church needs to find a way to reestablish in the consciousness of its people the separate and inestimable values of ordained priesthood and of celibate chastity, which are among the most ancient of all its traditional vocations.

This would allow us to project a renewed and joyous proclamation of the lived hope and magnanimous following of Jesus Christ that would ideally characterize the celibate chastity of those, including undoubtedly some ordained priests, whom the Spirit of God gifts with this charism. Here we might turn to those religious orders, of women and men, who have articulated this persuasively not only in their constitutions but even more movingly in the lives and persons of their members. We would need to hear, as well, the reflections of those ordained priests in every diocese whose lives and ministries manifest the tenderness and vitality of this special gift of God's Spirit among us.

*   *   *   *   *

Celibacy that is God-given and sustained is a gift that enriches the life of the person who is called to it. It is then a blessing for the Church. The celibate person gives a particular kind of witness to the all-embracing love of our God in Jesus Christ and offers testimony to the truth that there is a fullness and depth of life beyond what we can see and to which all of us are called. It is a witness in faith to the final times when we will not be given or received in marriage but will be embraced in the Love that transcends and incorporates all loving human relationships.

In addition, celibacy that is really lived and not simply endured makes a powerful countercultural statement in today's world. In these latter years of the twentieth century we have witnessed in our nation a development that often regards sexual activity as a casual, recreational, taken-for-granted activity rather than as an expression of spiritual values and a pledge of love and commitment to another person. Consequently, the message seen and heard so often is that a person who is a virgin for whatever reason is a person who is missing one of the essentials of life and should therefore be pitied or held up to scorn. The pressures to engage in premarital and extramarital sexual activity are quite strong in many circles of today's society.

The witness of a person who is celibate by vocation and choice and who leads a life marked by significant, loving relationships and productive service makes a strong contribution to those who struggle to find a sense of their own dignity and worth. They can see in such a person one who in a particular way needs to depend on the loving providence of a merciful God and who needs to be in good touch with the mainstreams of his or her own inner life.

In such a person they can find an example of the kind of interior freedom and regard for others that allows a person to share and to discover life through loving, effective, substantial relationships with a variety of people. And they can note this generativity happening without benefit either of marriage or genital sexual activity.

I want to underscore the fact that while the celibate person refrains from marriage and from genital sexual activity, it is not these renunciations alone which give heart to a life of celibacy and make it an effective way of loving in the Spirit of Christ. Merely to abstain from such relationships and activity says little to people unless the abstention gives birth in the celibate persons to the kind of serving, loving relationships I mentioned above. Most of us have known people, and perhaps have edged toward this disposition ourselves, who, while not married or sexually active, have no human relationships of any apparent warmth, depth, or significance. To the extent that this is the case with priests, they tend to be withdrawn or antagonistic, or work driven or addicted or sterile in their approach to ministry. Whatever they may be in their heart of hearts they are not seen as people who are involved in a fruitful way of loving or who are expansive or inviting or compassionate or understanding of the human struggles of the people they are ordained to serve. When this occurs, it is painful and disappointing to the community and to the celibate person who ends up in such a constricted state. One would never deliberately and consciously choose such a condition. To find oneself in it has to be a dreadfully painful experience.

No, the celibate priest needs to have a variety of significant relationships in his life if his mode of being is to bear some resemblance to that of Jesus Christ and if he is to be a witness to a way of love that is personally life giving and appealing to others. For this reason I judge it to be vitally important that seminary communities not be physically or spiritually remote from the motions and currents of daily living nor that they be composed only of young men studying for the priesthood. I understand that there is a need in seminary years for some peace and quiet, for courses of a particular nature and quality, for good solid interaction between those aspiring to ordination and those already ordained. But when these necessary values are realized at the expense of other important relationships, I believe that we are being very short-sighted.

Seminarians are generally enriched when they share their years of theological study with both female and male lay students. In the normal course of events, such students are older and bring to the theological enterprise a breadth of experience and a sense of commitment that can only enrich the seminarians. And I honestly believe that candidates for priesthood are impoverished if they have not had some women as professors, counselors, and spiritual guides.

I say that because it is impossible for an ordained priest to be an effective pastoral minister in today's Church if he is unable or unwilling to serve with or sometimes under the direction of lay women and men who in greater numbers are devoting their lives to Church ministry. And, apart from the call to ministerial colleagueship, today's priest needs to respond to the call of the community to enter into real, human relationships with them, the women as well as the men, if he is to have any real hope of being a credible minister among them. It seems to me that the day is long gone when a priest can be above or otherwise remote from the community he is called to serve. He needs to serve as a pilgrim among pilgrims, not as one who has already arrived and now coaches or instructs others how to negotiate the road.

Another circumstance of the day that calls the priest to varied, significant relationships in the community is the decreasing number of ordained priests in the Church. Not many years ago, priests, especially in their earlier years, could expect to live with at least one other priest and often enough with two or three others. It was then the fond aspiration of most to be off on their own or to be pastors of smaller parishes where, generally, they were the only priest in residence. Now, most priests live with other priests for only a few years. More and more are finding this a hardship. Indeed, the tendency now is for priests involved in a variety of ministries to seek ways to share at least a common table, if not a common residence, for mutual support and encouragement.

As years go by and we experience cultural shifts and renewed theological understandings, our pastoral practices change as well. We need to honor the lasting values and deepest truths of our faith. We best do that when we proclaim it and symbolize it in ways that touch the human heart and help people come to deeper life. All of us have experienced many such shifts in our lifetime. We know that we have welcomed some with ease and others with difficulty. And we realize that what may have been a joyful change for one person could well have been quite painful for another.

* * * * *

Who knows with certainty what the future holds for us with reference to celibacy and the ordained priesthood?

My judgment is that we need to take a long, loving look at the priesthood, which is taking new shape and new direction in so many of the local Churches. I think that what is happening is a sign of vitality, and I trust that the Holy Spirit will guide us as we seek to exercise the ministerial priesthood in today's Church in ways that speak to people's hearts and nourish their faith. But I believe that the Holy Spirit does not move apart from the hard work, wit, creativity, and holy imagination with which God endows all persons in the Church. For this reason I am convinced that bishops need to listen to their priests and their people about what lends deepest sig-

nificance to their experience of priesthood in today's Church.
I do believe that the Holy See would do the whole Church
a great service if it invited the bishops of the world to engage
in that kind of dialogue and then invited them to share their
findings.

My intuition is that we would discover a widespread and
growing conviction that while our people honor deeply the
tradition of celibacy in the Church, they are concerned that
we are overemphasizing its importance. That is a concern that
I hear every day and it is a concern that I share. I honor
celibacy as a beautiful gift of the Holy Spirit for the good of
the Church. At the same time I am aware that requiring it
in the ordained priest is a human construct, which by all evidence available to me is gradually diminishing the Church's
capacity to celebrate its Eucharistic life.

The Priest and Social Justice

Rembert G. Weakland, O.S.B., D.D.

On December 7, 1965, two documents were promulgated at Vatican Council II, the Decree on the Ministry and Life of Priests and the Pastoral Constitution on the Church in the Modern World. In reading them in sequence, one is led to believe that they came out of two different mind-sets. The first says nothing about how the priest is to relate to the world, so that many of the urgent issues that are touched upon in the second document are not even mentioned in the account of the priest's roles and tasks. For example, how the priest should relate to economic questions, to marriage and its central position in our society, to the quest for peace in the world, to politics, are not dealt with. The second document tells us, however, that all of these questions are very much a part of the mission of the Church. Even though the first document says that the priest and his specific ministry are essential to the full mission of the Church, there are so many social areas where his specific role is not even brought up in the council documents. If the Church has a role, should not the priest also have one?

The latest revision of the Code of Canon Law rectifies this lacuna somewhat by stating among the duties of the pastor that "he is to foster works by which the spirit of the Gospel, including issues involving social justice, is promoted" (can. 528, no. 1). Nevertheless, there is some hesitancy on the part of some priests to enter into the fray. They see confreres of theirs picketing before abortion clinics or speaking at peace rallies or even engaging in civil disobedience at nuclear arms plants, and they feel guilty lest they appear less courageous, less authentically Christian. Somehow they do not feel that explicit actions of this sort are necessarily a part of their priestly mission and calling. They do believe that working for social justice is a constitutive part of living the gospel, but they have so many hesitations on how that is to be realized for them in the concrete. Often they admire their fellow priests who are activists and wish they could be so convinced and single-minded. But it just is not that way for themselves.

Hesitations

The first serious hesitation that a priest today often expresses is that he really does not know Catholic social teaching and is not comfortable talking about it. He will tell you that when he was in the seminary after World War II or even up till the seventies there was no consistent course on Catholic social teaching nor was it a priority in the curriculum. He may have heard about the role of the labor priests in the thirties and later, but labor issues were not as real to him as they had been to a previous generation of priests who came from blue-collar families where members were very involved in union activity. He also has many negative views and hesitations about the labor unions and knew the stories of massive corruption in their highest ranks that had often filled the newspapers. All of this leaves him with a feeling of preferring to avoid the whole arena.

Moreover, he will tell you that if he enters into this question of social justice in his sermons, he turns off half of his congregation. Many of them are people from immigrant parents or grandparents who worked their way up to higher places in the corporate world of the U.S.A. with many sacrifices and much effort. They did what they had been told to do during their years of education in a Catholic grade school, in a Catholic high school, and finally in a Catholic college: that is, study hard and get ahead. Now that they have done this they feel that they are being told by their priests that they have given in to materialism and consumerism. They do not want to be put on a guilt trip because of success.

Priests know that if they preach about social justice they will be accosted after Mass and told by some that politics do not belong in the pulpit. Our American tradition is that of separation of Church and state. We have come to resent any overtly political talk in the pulpit. Although we know, unfortunately, that this division has led some to the point of affirming that there is no religious or ethical content to political issues and we are unhappy about this turn of events, still we do not know how to approach issues so as to avoid dividing our faith community.

The problem becomes more complicated when what we say is labeled as favoring either the Democratic or the Republican platform. We are very, very sensitive to the use of the pulpit in a way that would favor one party over another. We prefer to say nothing about an issue rather than to get in the squabble between parties.

Lastly, even when a priest knows fairly well Catholic social teaching and its history and is able to explain it, he may hesitate in making particular applications to the situation today because of the incredible amount of information one must have to make any kind of knowledgeable judgment. The information is changing so rapidly, and one has only the newspapers to rely on; there is always the feeling that the situation has changed before we get around to relating it to the teaching we know. Going from the abstract principles we learned in the seminary to concrete cases that we encounter in the lives of our parishioners is not easy. There are many pitfalls along the way. We only have to make fools of ourselves once to decide not to get involved again.

Sometimes I hear laypeople say that priests do not speak out on urgent social issues because they do not want to lose the contributions of their wealthy members who would be offended. This may be the case in some instances, but I do not feel that it happens that often. Nevertheless, we are all vulnerable to such pressures, even when they are subtle and indirect. In a diocese or in a parish one could become a slave, as it were, to the donations of a few. There may well arise the occasion when one must take a stand regardless of the consequences and the financial loss it entails.

We must also admit that we are the victims of our own cultural environment. Most of us come from upper-middle-class families with the values that surround that class. Our values come from our families, from television, from the newspapers. Seldom do we spend time analyzing how those values—or disvalues—affect our own actions as well as those around us. We often say things like: But I do not have the vow of poverty; I'm no religious. I have to think of my old age too. I really needed that vacation in Jamaica. And probably we did, but we still feel guilty because we sense that our people might be a bit scandalized by our own values or lack of them. We hesitate to preach Catholic social teaching because we sense we might seem hypocritical, since we are no exemplars ourselves.

Extremes to Be Avoided

If we were asked the question: Does the gospel message have anything to do with the way we act in this world and the way in which people should relate in society, I am sure we would at once answer yes. We do not have any doubts about the fact that the gospel is clear: Discipleship means more than lip service; it also involves action. We would even say that it also involves the structures of society under which we live, whether they make it easier or more difficult to be a Christian. We would avoid the extreme of thinking that the mission of the Church—a continuation of the mission of Jesus Christ—is a purely spiritual one. We know instinctively that such a distinction between gospel and society that would make them totally unrelated areas cannot be right. It is not traditional Catholicism; such an attitude cannot be squared with the teachings of Jesus.

Such a spiritualization, however, has more subtle forms. Frequently during debates on the economic pastoral letter of the United States bishops, *Economic Justice for All*, I would be confronted with the assertion that the role of the Church is to save souls and not to meddle in worldly affairs about which the Church knows nothing. Saving souls is indeed the mission of the Church, but people save their souls in this world, that is, by living lives according to the precepts of the gospel, and those gospel commandments say much about how to relate to the world here and now. One does not save one's soul by jumping over this world, but by living in this world according to the commands of Jesus Christ—commands of love that involve how one relates to others on every level. Saint John's letters are quite clear on that point. One begs the question, then, to say that saving souls is the mission of the Church, as if such saving took place outside and without relationship to this world here and now.

There is an opposite extreme that must be avoided: It could be called the social gospel. It is a tendency to reduce the mission of Jesus Christ and, thus, of the Church to bettering the lot of all on this globe, as if the prime task of the Church were a social one. A theory of this sort tends to equate social progress with God's kingdom being realized. It makes no distinction between the inner workings of grace that could rest very invisible and outward social progress. Such a theory is a great temptation for us Americans. We tend to need clear signs of progress and achievement by which to measure our accomplishments. We are reluctant to leave to God the task of assessing our accomplishments in terms of Church mission.

God's freedom must always be protected; the kingdom belongs to God, not to us. It will take shapes we could not dream of. God writes with crooked lines, never according to our limited human ways. God must be left to act as God. We tend to want to denude God's way of all mystery, to humanize it, to control it, to encapsulate it. None of that is possible. God must be given the freedom to be God and surprise us. No social plans or programs, regardless of how efficient or effective, are to be automatically equated with God's kingdom.

Moreover, to equate human social progress with the kingdom is materialism in its worst form. It fails to take into account the role of grace as a free and unmerited gift of God that sanctifies. No sanctification can be gained by our own earthly merit, regardless of how creative and original and good it may seem to us. A temptation to think in this fashion is always there and must be avoided. Some have criticized liberation theology for falling at times into this temptation, as if progress in human welfare were the mission of the Church and the determinant of the kingdom. Taken in this kind of unqualified way, one would have to say that it does not hold up as being a part of the teaching of Jesus. If overspiritualization is a false path, so is overemphasis on social progress as being identified with God's kingdom, even though there is a bit of truth in both tendencies.

The last extreme that must be avoided is that of pulling one issue out of all the social concerns and making it the test for the whole. We talk of single-issue people. We mean by that that they so overexaggerate the importance of one social concern that it becomes the criterion by which all the others are judged. It becomes so all-absorbing that other issues in practice do not seem to count. Perhaps it is easier to experience such Christians than to describe them. They are never content with what you do as priest since they feel you must do more. They say yes when you talk about a consistent ethic of life but then take you right back to their particular issue as if the others did not exist. In the flow and ebb of life, single-issue people never know how to balance several issues that are of importance. They see this as compromise, a dirty word that means capitulation.

We all have known single-issue people and do not want to become that way. Our way out is often to avoid all social issues; that way we are safe.

We also are afraid that single-issue people seem to distort information, denigrate those who may not agree with them and act in a way very contrary to the discipleship of Christ. We do not want to become that way and so would prefer to avoid social issues altogether.

In spite of all these negative aspects that must be avoided one must still say that Catholic social teaching has been an important part of our heritage and one that must be safeguarded. We must reflect on the role of the priest with regard to social issues if the priest's role in the total mission of the Church is to be complete.

It is clearly a part of the priest's mission to see that the extremes just cited do not become a part of his teaching or example.

I would like now to treat of some of the more positive aspects of this part of the priest's ministry. The priest's first task is that of a teacher and proclaimer of God's word.

The Priest as Teacher

The first attitude that the priest must have is the conviction that all aspects of this world are important for the kingdom of God. Another way of expressing this idea is to say that everything that is and that happens in this world is important to God and a part of the divine plan. We can omit for the sake of brevity how God relates to evil through permitting it—that subject consumed tomes full of rationalizing arguments in the Middle Ages. One can say, however, with certain assurance that God can derive good even out of evil events. Or one can say that nothing can hinder God from bringing to fulfillment the kingdom that began with Jesus Christ.

Such a positive perspective follows from the fact that God entered human history with the birth of Jesus Christ. That breaking into our existence of the divine colors everything that is and that happens. All of human history takes on a new dimension beyond what can be seen by human eyes. Human history must be seen now from the divine point of view.

Yet we must also say that the complete fulfillment of the kingdom comes only at the end of time. It will happen when and as God wills. In that way we do not equate the kingdom just with our own acts and feeble attempts at goodness. But God does not jump over this world in building the kingdom. What happens here and now is the stuff out of which the kingdom is made. This world and its history are intimately entwined with God's plans for the kingdom. In this concept we can place great value on what happens on this earth and human history. We can also say that what happens here in some way or another is a part of God's kingdom and will ultimately make sense because of that participation in the destiny God has for this world.

It is also true that each one of us, being as we are unique and different, makes the kingdom of God in its ultimate state different. We add by our very being to what the kingdom is and will be. That should not make us proud, just aware of the fact that God has indeed chosen us out of infinite love and goodness to be a part of the divine plan. Of course, it gives us all an infinite dignity and worth that goes beyond just being human.

The reason why this basic attitude is important for the personal life of the priest and for his teaching is his task to help all the baptized overcome the tendency of seeing some aspects of life as somehow outside the realm of religious significance. Sometimes people engaged in business affairs will give this impression, as if there is some sphere that runs, as it were, on its own without any reference to God and the divine. We tend to fall into dichotomies such as secular and sacred, as if this distinction meant that we could classify everything as belonging to one category or another. From God's point of view, everything is important and a part of creation and redemption. I might add that this attitude today is more important than ever before as we seek to find an adequate theology for the ecological concerns that are ours.

The term used by Vatican Council II in the Pastoral Constitution on the Church in the Modern World is "compenetration." The sacred city and the secular city grow up together in one history.

We see in the life of Jesus, for example, that he was often moved to pity by human suffering and cured it. He did not say that he came only for spiritual healing. Note the parable of the paralytic; he also used the physical cure to show that he had the power to heal spiritually as well. The two are not so easily separated in the life of Jesus Christ.

The priest must preach and demonstrate this attitude toward the world. God is found, for most people, in the ordinary events and happenings of life. These events become the fodder for reflection on God and this world. God is to be found there, even when the presence of God is hard to discern. But the basic attitude is one of being fully engaged with and in this world and not—as in some kind of nirvana—trying to escape from it.

But he can do more than just teach about this importance of the world in the fulfillment of God's kingdom; he can also teach about the signs of the kingdom here and now, about what human society should be like when God's presence fills it. In other words, his teaching can also be positive and lead to action.

Signs of the Kingdom

What are the signs when God is active among the people? One only has to read the Bible to answer that question. The priest as teacher must help people to recognize those signs of the kingdom. More than that, the priest must be a spiritual leader helping the entire community to cooperate with the Holy Spirit in bringing forth those signs of the kingdom. It is possible, for example, to begin with the old covenant and preach about the way God worked wonders in saving the people, as a way of entering into this theme. The saving power of God as seen in the Old Testament gives the priest-teacher a wonderful opportunity to help the faithful see the power of God's love in action.

The choicest texts, however, for preaching about the signs of the kingdom are the prophets, especially Isaiah. The visions of Isaiah about the future when God would again be active among the people become vivid signs of the kingdom. We see the poor, in particular, having the gospel preached to them. We find justice in the land. We find peace as well. All those texts that show what happens to God's people when the power of God's presence and creative Spirit is at work are important for describing the nature of God's kingdom even now.

Many will say, of course, that these texts describe a utopia that cannot be realized. The "real" world just does not work that way. How often I have heard that comment! There is a difference between utopias and visions. Utopias may be make-believe and ignore the effects of evil within society and on human beings. In that respect they can be illusionary and perhaps even dangerous. But we all need vision (dreams) about how reality could be; we all need to have before us ideals to strive after. These texts may never be totally realizable in the here and now, but they tell us that if we cooperate with God's freely given graces and gifts, we can go beyond our mere human aspirations and expectations. These dreams and visions of the prophets are not tricks of the imagination but ways of seeing God's plan for the human family and this earth, realizable through God's own power and presence.

In the New Testament we see similar visions worked out by Jesus, especially in the Sermon on the Mount. The Beatitudes give a similar attitude toward life and toward God's presence in our lives. They become ways of helping us be like Christ himself. The priest must make these visions of Jesus Christ—visions of people who follow the commandments of love of God and neighbor—ideals to be striven after. He, too, tells us that his legacy to us is peace—like that described by Isaiah. It is the kind of peace that comes about when all is working in harmony. It is the image of the lion lying down with the lamb that is evoked by Isaiah.

Jesus also talks about the charity that should animate our relations with others. It is the kind of unselfishness that he showed in his own life. The Gospel of John is the story of that love lived out. His epistles are that same love exemplified in the Christian community. The descriptions of the first communities of Jerusalem are nothing more than this ideal striven for on a daily basis.

Paul and Acts carry forward for us these ideals and show how the fledgling communities wherever they were founded faced the world they lived in with the new zeal of their acquired faith. They act also for us as models against which we can test our own zeal in being a part of the kingdom with all the joys and sufferings such discipleship entails.

Working for peace at all levels is a sign of the kingdom. Acts of charity are a sign of the kingdom. Striving for justice for all, especially for the poor and the strangers, is a sign of God's caring presence in our midst and, thus, of the kingdom.

Each time the priest as preacher and teacher talks of these values of the kingdom and tries to help the faithful live them out in their daily concerns, he is assisting the faithful to play their role in bringing about the kingdom.

The most difficult aspect of preaching and teaching about the kingdom centers on the distinction between charity and justice. We find ourselves comfortable in preaching about charity. It is easy to see that helping others according to our abilities is a Christian duty. We do not do enough charity, we do not share enough with others of our bounty—and, as Pope John Paul has told us—of our substance. In spite of these lapses of ours, at least we do not fight the principle of charity. We all admire Mother Teresa. She is in our day the perfect example of this Christian virtue. We can so easily praise those organizations that are involved in charitable works—Saint Vincent de Paul, for example.

But it is much more difficult for us to enter into the area of justice. The people of the Old Testament must have lived so very often in societies that were unjust, because they are always talking about the need for justice. The poor and the widow were exploited; judges were dishonest. To talk of justice was a necessary duty for the prophets. Jesus was concerned for these same disenfranchised; he demonstrated a special love for the poor. He was harsh in his words toward the religious leaders who exploited others.

His Sermon on the Mount showed his sense of the worth and dignity of every person. He told the lowly how God had each hair of their heads numbered. Justice must be founded on the dignity and worth of each, a dignity and worth to be constantly respected by all. The freeing up that Jesus did by his healings and by casting out evil spirits shows that he wanted each person to be as God had created each one. The value of the person is shown by helping them to be freed from all bondage. The priest must help every one enter into the dynamic of these concepts. The parable of the Good Samaritan stretches us in our relationships to others. Charity and duty coincide. One almost sees this reaching out as a part of being ''just'' in the full biblical sense.

If there are shackles in our society that keep people from being free and from having the opportunities of being who they were intended to be by God, then we must work toward a just society where the potential of all can be realized.

All social justice and action begin by realizing the worth and dignity of each person because of being created to the image and likeness of God, before any consideration of race, sex, accomplishments, family ties, or external power. The priest must continue to preach this worth and help the faithful see that it embraces all on this globe without exception.

On the one hand, most of us are comfortable with works of charity but less at ease when it comes to being involved in works of justice. On the other hand, how we vote in every election says much about how we view justice in our society. It says much about our priorities. It is not necessary to be out on picket lines to make a statement or to participate; we are doing so constantly by our choices. In fact, I am one who believes that often the more strident means of demonstrating bring the opposite effect hoped for. We also strive for justice by the many causes we support with our pocketbooks and with our time. This style of changing society through voluntary organizations, a process that is so much a part of the fabric of our American society, gives us ample occasion in unostentatious ways of doing our share to make our society and this world better.

We and our people must be convinced that every time we act charitably toward those in need we bring forth a sign of the kingdom of God and help to realize the kingdom here and now. Every time we act justly toward others and seek with them their justice we help realize the kingdom and help others to see God's active presence among us.

A very difficult but important task of the priest is to show his people how the liturgy, and especially the Mass, is by its very nature a vehicle for creating a community of charity and justice. The sacraments by the very nature of their being are communal; that is, they are the action of the whole community assembled. They are to bring about what they signify, namely, unity with Christ and among all assembled on the level of divine love. There is no such thing as a private sacrament. They are very personal in that they are to change our very being, but they are always the work of the whole community.

This aspect of the liturgy and especially of the Mass is realized most clearly during the Mass on Holy Thursday. The very meaning of Eucharist is there presented as service to others and especially to the poor. The washing of the feet is but a symbol of the larger meaning of Eucharist. Saint Paul had rightly scolded the Corinthians for not understanding this deeper meaning of Eucharist. No one can participate in the Eucharist over and over again without being aware of the unity with others that it effects. That unity, as Saint John knew, has to be expressed then in love in action. The Eucharist does not end with the final blessing at Mass; it must continue to permeate the life of each baptized. I knew that the liturgical renewal was on the right track when a banker of some prominence told me that he had become a much better banker—from a discipleship point of view—by becoming a Eucharistic minister. He was able rightly to connect this liturgical ministry with its ultimate aim of sustaining those who minister in the world.

We have been somewhat successful in teaching our people this communal aspect of some of the sacraments such as Eucharist, in some cases reconciliation, in the new rite of the anointing of the sick, and sometimes confirmation. We have failed miserably with marriage. There is still much to be taught in the area of sacraments to help our people see that they are meant to sustain us as members of a community in our ministries to the world.

The Vocation of the Laity

Each of the baptized has a role to play in God's kingdom. For the laity that role, for the most part, is played out in the world. "World" here means home, work, and society with its multiple relationships. Each person must work with the gifts, talents, deficiencies, handicaps, and graces they receive to bring about the kingdom through the action of the Holy Spirit. The priest must help the laity see that their role is precisely to bring the values of the kingdom preached by Jesus Christ to the world in which they live and work. The laity are the primary evangelizers.

This concept is most important today when there is a tendency to see the laity as focusing inward toward needed ministries within the Church. Although those ministries are important to the life of the Church and fostered as such, they are not the primary task of the laity; they are indeed exceptions and very limited in number when one sees the mission of all the members of the Church taken as a whole. It is not the role of the priest to assume this role of the laity in the world. His task is to encourage and instruct the laity, not take their roles from them. It is perfectly sound judgment for a priest to say that he does not belong in a picket line; he should not feel guilty about letting the laity do their ministry to the world.

The parish should be supportive of all these lay roles in the world. We have done a splendid job of making our parishes centers for specialized ministry to many hurting groups in the world—divorced, handicapped, grieving, and the like; but we have not been supportive of those who have a very clear task in the kingdom being realized out there. I think, for example, of the lack of support for those in politics, in business, in law enforcement, in health care, in the communications media, in teaching, in the arts. Often these people only see the Church as a place to go to on Sunday for an hour. They have come to expect little more than an occasional nod in their direction when the Church needs their free services. They are, however, the Church in the world and must be supported as such.

At times these laity in the world must also be challenged. Often they seem to act no differently than others in the values they project. Challenging is a part of the priest's ministry; it is not restricted just to teaching and preaching consoling words. The prophets of the Old Testament cannot be read at Mass and commented on without the laity being challenged, at times forcefully. At the same time, people do get tired of being nagged. Bringing them to new heights of awareness about the demands of discipleship is a part of being priest.

It would be my advice to the priest that he must preach the word of God and let it challenge without becoming stri-

dent and obnoxious, judgmental and personal. He must give
the vision of a better world and encourage all to cooperate
to build it and increase signs of the kingdom that give so much
hope to those in need. He must encourage all to do works
of charity and stimulate them to go beyond the easy charity
of just sharing what one has left over or can take a tax deduc-
tion on. He must encourage the laity to be involved in social
action through the many organizations that our society so
easily produces.

All of that is clear. One difficult and vital question remains
to be treated. How involved should the Church as parish or
as faith community be in both charity and social action?

My sage advice is that we can without too much trouble
be very much involved as Church and as parish and not just
as individuals when it comes to actions that would rightly be
classified as acts of charity. One would expect that of Church
and church groups. In fact, the churches are probably the best
voluntary organizations for such works. They have the experience and skills needed for helping others. Often the charitable work must be accompanied by other signs of hope so
that the people in need can gain the incentives needed to face
life anew. The Church has been very effective—note the
Catholic school system and the history of the immigrant groups
that came to the United States in the last century and early
part of this century—in giving to those not yet making it a
sense of well being, of dignity and worth, so that they could
obtain the skills to be independent. Charity is an easy question in terms of not just personal but also community or parish action.

Social action issues are much more difficult for us as
Church to work with. We almost immediately at this junc-
ture of history fall into two classes according to our political
affiliation when it comes to what specific action must be taken.
Here the priest has a more difficult time of it. He must be
able to help the community state clearly the problem. He must
help the group work on the solutions without permitting the

community to split into party politics. There are, however, issues where such a split is less likely to take place, and these are perhaps the best to start with. So, for example, the question of pornography and its moral implications are very well agreed upon. I do not know of a split between parties over that issue. It degrades women and children in every way and works against human dignity.

I believe we should also be able to agree on the fundamental equality of all people and fight together against racism and sexism. We can agree on the pursuit of nonviolent strategies on all levels of society. The pursuit of nonviolence is much needed in our cities and in the world. We must also agree on the esteem needed for sexual integrity, fidelity, and stability in marital life and family. We could well work together on antirape. We should also be able to work together without party splits on questions that affect future generations, especially responsible stewardship for this planet.

Perhaps the more difficult issues can also be attacked and some agreement reached on their moral implications, even if agreement on modes of making the situation better cannot be at once achieved. These issues touch the lives of those on welfare and other entitlements. I believe all would agree on the values of dignity and worth and the need to help people be independent of state handouts. Achieving that agreement is important, even if there is diversity of views as to the actions to be pursued. Even here we could agree that solutions must not only respect the dignity of each and weigh the proposed solutions in that light, but we could also agree that the proposals for action must strengthen and not weaken family life. That aspect could also become a litmus test of our values applied to specific cases. I also believe that there is more agreement on the morality of abortion than some might have us believe. We could well avoid splitting—this time not on party lines—on the question of any exceptions to the Church's absolute teaching and get down to the business of seeing how the number of abortions can be reduced. I did not find any

Catholic woman or man defending abortion as a moral good for society or as a desired solution to problems.

In all the above it is not necessary for the entire parish to agree on a common course of action, but discussion on the issues from the point of view of the values cited can help all to take their responsible place in the world as disciples of Christ. The priest's role in handling all of these issues is to keep God's point of view clearly before the eyes of all, to keep unity in the community, and to challenge everyone not to take the easy road of neglect or discouragement.

Catholic Social Teaching

In the above, I have approached the role of the priest and his teaching mostly from the biblical perspective. It seems to me that this approach is more akin to where our people are today. However, the whole body of Catholic social teaching can be useful to the priest in his ministry if properly used. I sense, however, that so many of the documents in the history of our social teaching are no longer of vital importance to the people. They treated of issues that are not important in our day. The priest should know them and something about the historical circumstances that brought them about without having to make all the faithful experts in them. They are not easy to read and could readily force people to become bored. There are, however, several principles that are the rockbed, as it were, of that teaching that need to be reemphasized today.

The whole question of rights that was raised by the Enlightenment had to be dealt with by the Church. The first right that was accepted was that of the principle of private property as against the tendency toward collectivism. These rights were based on the principle of personal dignity and worth. The rights of workers were next considered, with strong emphasis on the right to form associations and to bargain for just wages and the right to proper working conditions. These questions of the rights of workers still form the basis of so much of Catholic social teaching. They are important questions, even if in today's world and in Catholic circles these issues seem to have taken a secondary role.

Against the backdrop of centralization on the part of the state—statism—Catholic social teaching evolved a concept of decentralization that goes under the term "subsidiarity." It postulates the principle that what can be done at a lower level should not be usurped by those at a higher level within the social fabric. Subsidiarity could be derived also from the principle of dignity and value of each individual and of the importance of primary associations of people. The whole list of rights was presented by Pope John XXIII, and these rights have been repeated subsequently by many popes. It is interesting today that it is the Church that has become the strongest voice in support of these rights and their extension to the unborn as well.

Since Catholic social teaching arose as responses to critical situations, it is not a logical and complete body of principles. It seems that each age has added to the doctrine by facing and reflecting on the critical social issues of that particular age. For this reason the body of doctrine will continue to grow. We, as Catholics, are not too used to such a process in our teaching and always want clear and total expositions of what is to be believed. For the most part in the past, Catholic social teaching not only arose out of concrete historical situations that affected negatively the lives of people but also responded more through the process of philosophical reflection on the natural law. It is only now that the biblical roots are being emphasized and explored. The pastoral letters of the American bishops are most helpful in seeing how that investigation has succeeded.

Our present pope, Pope John Paul, has added much to this corpus of teaching on social issues through his encyclicals. The important one early in his pontificate, On Human Labor, brought to their ultimate conclusions the principles laid down by previous popes. His most recent, On Social Concerns, brings the whole body of social teaching to bear on world issues. I would counsel the priest today that these world issues will form the substance of much of the social teaching that is yet to come because of the nature of our present economic and world structures.

It is, thus, important for the priest as teacher to keep the faithful alert to these issues and the reflections that are constantly taking place. For example, I expect that the next area of social doctrine that will come forth will have to deal with ecological questions and the relationship between human needs and the future of the globe.

Finally, the priest should not be nervous about being a part of the application of the gospel to social problems and injustices. We accept that we can make mistakes in all areas of our life and ministry and that there is forgiveness. We learn through our mistakes. But in the area of social justice we somehow seem to feel that every effort must be perfect. We all know that we have been "taken" when it comes to charity. We smile and chalk it up to experience. In the realm of social action we must also learn by experience and make our mistakes. Bad judgment can be rectified.

In the midst of all the trying problems of our age the priest must be a sign and herald of hope to the faithful. They, too, have a right to make their mistakes and to learn from them. When all of our solutions and efforts seem to be of no avail, the priest must also help us fall on our knees in prayer that we have the insights and wisdom needed to find an answer. Social action, charity, and all works of the kingdom must be the outcome of prayer. We learn that we are weak and imperfect instruments whom God surprisingly uses to build the kingdom. We should constantly be in admiration of this trust and confidence in our ability to respond to God's call. The priest should be the leader in such trust in God's providence.

I Invite You to Accompaniment

Donna M. Hanson

Dear David,

Your Dad and I were delighted to have you home from college for spring break. Attending the Easter Vigil with us and celebrating our traditional family dinner were especially meaningful to me. With just your senior year remaining before you are at graduate school, Dad and I look forward to at least one more Easter gathering, baskets, bunnies, and all.

David, since you returned to school, our discussions about priesthood have been very much on my mind. The insights you offered the night before you left continue to challenge me. During the Easter octave, my thinking was also impacted by the gospel reading of the Emmaus journey. Jesus was the stranger who *accompanied* the two disciples as they walked the seven miles from Jerusalem and "came to know him in the breaking of the bread." With all of these thoughts whirling around in my head, I wanted to continue our dialogue with one of my long, reflective letters.

As you and I discussed priesthood and I thought about the strangers who have touched our lives, I saw so many parallels between priesthood and parenting. Both are a journey into the unknown that is profoundly impacted by our earlier life experiences. Perhaps an illustration of my expectations about parenting that accompanied me into adulthood will be helpful.

As I grew up, I subconsciously accepted the philosophy that was followed by my parents and supported by the Church and society. It seemed to be that parents had to have the answers for all questions and the rules to govern every situation. Otherwise, we children would not respect them and the limits they established. As our firstborn, you were my "hands on" teacher about parenting. I quickly learned that not only was I lacking all of the answers, many times I also needed to listen very carefully before I could really understand your questions. Our accompaniment, including my letting go of unreal expectations and your sharing words of wisdom, permitted me to become far more than a dispenser of rules.

From my own early parenting days, one of my more vivid memories is walking through a department store complex when you were almost four years old and your brother Steve just two. Steve was sitting in the shopping cart and you were walking along beside me, I thought. Hearing a thunderous crash, I whirled around just in time to see a mannequin's head roll down the aisle, an arm crash at my feet, and a wig come to rest on the counter a short distance away. You looked wide-eyed at me and said, "Mom, how can you learn about things if you cannot feel them?"

For twenty-one years now, I have been feeling things differently because of you and Steve. With your honesty, integrity, and independence, you two have made me more reflective, more patient, and, I pray, more the person God calls me to be. As our family has spent time with priest friends and we have discussed priesthood and formation, you have expanded my thinking. In fact, you and Steve are the ones far more than I who will be the mainstay of the Church in the twenty-first century. If priesthood is not responsive to your generation, we will lose richness in our future and ultimately in our history and tradition.

David, in writing about priesthood, I do want to again acknowledge your "caveat." You said that the reason you do not feel attracted to the priesthood is because you want to have a family. I like to think that your own experience of family life has been so positive that you desire repeating it in adulthood! Whether or not that is the case, I know that the priests I have most admired over the years also would make wonderful husbands and fathers. In fact, I have come to question whether anyone who did not desire a family could be an effective priest. Having acknowledged your "given," our discussion now seems to be centering on two key areas: the personal qualities necessary for an effective priest; and the academic, spiritual, and pastoral elements of priestly formation.

Paraphrasing Jesus' words, you offered an excellent insight: "Priesthood requires changing the image of a shepherd herding around simple-minded sheep to that of a person who journeys with others as a compassionate servant." You described this priest as one to whom others can come for understanding and assistance. Not surprisingly, the attributes you sought were the same I would expect in any "good" person. You insightfully noted that, above all, a priest must be a person of integrity, a very secure individual who will not succumb to the trappings of power. Having people's individual attention when addressing a congregation each week and the open invitation into their lives is indeed a powerful position. It could easily turn one's head. Priest, religious, and laity all need to hear your caution.

At a personal level, I can identify with that temptation. I am sure you can remember when I chaired the National Advisory Council to the National Conference of Catholic Bishops. One day I attended their administrative board meeting to present a report. There were well over fifty bishops, archbishops, and cardinals at the meeting. I presented a twelve-page report, responded to some questions about the Synod on the Laity, and then caught a flight back to Spokane. After arriving, I drove your swim-team car pool, did some work at the office, and zipped home to prepare dinner. Afterwards, you, Steve, and Dad had other commitments, and I was left alone in the kitchen doing the dishes. As I stood at the sink, I began to feel depressed. I thought: "This morning I was in Washington, D.C.—the hub of power—giving what I hoped was significant advice to the leadership of the Catholic Church in the United States. What am I doing here tonight, scrubbing grease from the bottom of a pan?" At that moment, I laughed and cried as I thought, "All of us, including the bishops, need to touch more reality and scrub more pans."

The reality of the changing expectations of priesthood came to me in the comments of what a forty-year-old priest friend has experienced since entering the seminary. His imagery describes the priesthood from being a role set in concrete to becoming like clay at the potter's wheel to now being sand that can easily slip through the smallest of fingers.

As a woman-wife-mother, I deeply understand my priest friend's anxiety, because my roles have also been undergoing these same dramatic changes. When you and Steve were born, your Dad and I were truly hoping for two boys. Dad's five brothers and one sister make it easy to understand his preference. Though I could not articulate it at the time, I now recognize that I was intimidated by the prospect of rearing a daughter. I did not know if I could deal with the "super mom" expectations that were being thrust on me and at the same time nurture a young woman through the challenges that I was only beginning to understand.

David, I will never know how I might have responded to a daughter, but I have no question that the role expectations of a "super mom" or a "super priest" are very similar and very painful. They are alienating and destructive, if for no other reason than they are impossible to fulfill. However, I also recognize that some women and some priests are caught in the trap because of looking for security in role expectations that once were but that will never be again. We are both struggling with changing expectations within and outside ourselves. For me, it is a matter of hanging on to the values of the past while letting go of the nonessentials for the future.

This basic struggle was well illustrated for me during our research trip to the library last December. In order to locate our resources, I walked to the card catalogue and you went to the computer. While neither of us is actually comfortable with the other system, I intellectually know my need for the speed and flexibility of the computer, and you appreciate the mundane reliability of the Dewey system when there is a power failure. Qualities that can help both of us forge ahead are openness to grow and change, honesty with our own pain, sensitivity to those around us, and a good sense of humor.

David, accompanying you these last three years as you have pursued a liberal arts degree only affirms for me what an ideal academic background it is for a priest. Whether we look back into our history or ahead to the future, *a learning teacher* is my image for priesthood. Christ was a learning teacher: constantly taking people where they were, listening to them and then sharing insights about their journey.

With a more highly educated population and the information explosion, each one of us is challenged with the necessity of lifelong learning. In such an environment, the priest does not have to have all the answers but rather be the motivator, the enabler, the animator, the midwife. Even now, some parishioners have more education than the priest in even the traditional areas of Catholic doctrine, Sacred Scripture, and canon law. Rather than being a threat to the priest, the successful parish will be the place where all are empowered to share their gifts with the entire community. Yet even more than utilizing their professional expertise, the greater challenge will be to assist all people to connect daily life with the word of God. Recognizing that each of us has a share in God's wisdom, the highly educated as well as those without any degree, is something we are just beginning to appreciate.

I was deeply moved by an African-American liturgy celebrated by a Maryknoll missionary in Baltimore. Three people were asked to read the parable of the Good Samaritan, taking the roles of the narrator, the lawyer, and Jesus. After the reading, the congregation of two hundred broke into groups for faith-sharing and gospel reflection. Fifteen minutes later, the community reassembled, and a few of the people shared their insights. One woman spoke about her twenty-year addiction to drugs and alcohol, and how finally, with the help of other people, her life turned around. A middle-aged white man described how a black couple rescued him while trapped under his car, then ended with a dramatic question: "If our positions had been reversed, would I have been a Good Samaritan to the black couple?" In the telling of their stories, these people profoundly impacted the entire congregation. They had not only been allowed but encouraged to break open God's word; in so doing, they left a legacy of both hope and challenge.

David, there is another dimension to "the learning teacher" that you continually bring home to me. As you know, I have had eighteen years of Catholic education, have been a staff member or volunteer in Catholic Charities for twenty-six years, and have attended innumerable workshops and conferences on virtually every topic related to Church and social ministry. Yet I find that your questions challenge me to think at a deeper level. The answers, I am discovering, are requiring me to combine my head learning with my heart experiences.

The incident that stands out most in my mind is our conversation last August. You and I were home alone on a Friday evening. At dinner, you began talking to me about a special young lady. The conversation took a radical turn when you changed the focus by asking the complex question: "Mom, did you just accept the Church's teaching on premarital sex or did you really think it through for yourself?" If you recall, over the next two hours, we talked about some of the loves of my life and the decisions I had made. As we were finishing the conversation, you thanked me for taking the time to share and said how glad you were that I had thought things through for myself. You then trundled off to bed and fell sound asleep. I lay awake for hours wondering both what I had said and how it had been received.

From my parental perspective, if the priest of the twenty-first century is to be a learning teacher, a strong academic background will be vital. In our instant society, having someone with a sense of historical perspective and an understanding of values is crucial. At the same time, the academic preparation must be joined together with the intellectual security necessary to be an enabler who can listen, call forth, and empower the people with whom life intersects on a day-to-day basis.

David, while the intellectual formation is important in challenging a wide range of people, I consider the spiritual dimension the core of priesthood. Christ, both priest and victim, was not only God but in his humanity made the ultimate sacrifice in his effort to heal: He actually gave his life so that all people could be restored. The image for spiritual formation of those called to service through the ordained priesthood is that of Christ *the wounded healer*. He had all power but he was totally vulnerable. He knew and came to be known by his family and friends: With them, he came face to face with his own humanity.

Modeling the wounded healer, we priests and laity come to know who we are at our core by sharing ourselves with God, with our families, and with other men and women in authentically intimate relationships. In our American culture and with our pre–Vatican II role expectations of priesthood, such relationships have turned our preconceived notions upside down.

A few years ago I was talking with a bishop from the South about how all of us have a need for a support system in family and in close friendships. He mentioned that he had been blessed with a forty-five-year relationship that began in the seminary, continued through ordination, and flourished during the years of service, when one became a monsignor and the other a bishop. In 1983, it happened that cancer took the life of his friend. At his funeral homily, the bishop unashamedly said: "Over these forty-five years, my friend has always been the giver. He has supported me and loved me without reservation. He has always been there when I've needed him. I am really going to miss him. If I have been a good priest, a good bishop, in large measure the credit goes to him. We talked to each other weekly. We vacationed all over the world together. He let you, his friends, be my friends. Only with God's help will I make it alone.''

David, in the telling of his story, I have told you about a good person, a good priest, a good friend. He is not perfect, but more importantly, he is not afraid to admit his vulnerability and his dependence on God and on other people. Unfortunately, some other priests whom I know do not have someone with whom they can share at their core. Unlike Christ, who had both male and female friends, a Lazarus and a Mary Magdalene, they do not have anyone to walk with them, work with them, and weep with them.

Turning it around, our family life has been deeply enriched because we have had priest friends who have truly journeyed with us. At our twenty-fifth wedding anniversary, the priest who had witnessed our marriage was with us as we renewed our vows. He has ''walked'' with Dad and me as you and Steve were born, as my Mom and Dad were buried, and as your graduations have occurred. When Steve asked him if he would come to his wedding whenever and wherever it occurs, he responded: ''Of course! Someone will have to keep your mother calm!''

This priest knows me well. He hired me out of graduate school, was there when I was installed as Director of Catholic Charities, and was the first person with whom I discussed the invitation to address Pope John Paul II. He came with us to the San Francisco Cathedral, and he organized my birthday celebration immediately after the presentation. He greeted me with the comment, ''Everything you have ever done came together today.'' He also helped pick up the pieces when one of the priests complimented me on the presentation and then asked, ''Did it cost our diocese an arm and a leg for you to participate?'' Over the years he has indeed walked with me, worked with me and wept with me.

David, perhaps the greatest similarity between priesthood and parenting is that they both require a total commitment. As you know, both you and Steve were delivered by Caesarean section. From those pregnancies, I know what it is to be willing to lay down one's life for another. However, after having someone totally dependent on you, it is terribly hard to let go. I see the parallel now occurring in priesthood as laity seek to achieve true equality, full participation, and rich inclusiveness. Again, Jesus gives both us parents and priests a model for imitation: it is that of *an enabling servant.*

During his time on earth, Jesus invited people to look within themselves to find solutions to the social, political, economic, and religious questions of the day. He built bridges by breaking down barriers in the process of community building. He was inclusive. He invited all to participate, and he treated each individual with true equality. When that community was formed, he celebrated one Eucharist, and he challenged us to do the same in memory of him.

Perhaps an example from our life will best illustrate my point. You and Steve often talk about Christmas Eve being your favorite night of the year. With our family tradition of gathering all the Hanson clan—brothers and sisters-in-law, children, grandmother, and now, as marriages occur, cousins-in-law—we have not only managed to maintain family ties but to experience community as well. Over the years, only as you have matured and I have become more comfortable with myself, have I really welcomed you, Steve, and Dad into the fullness of the celebration. Whereas I once thought I had to do everything so that it would be a perfect evening, I now know that in the preparations we become a closer family. Our relatives also find not perfection but a warm, inviting place where no one is overburdened and everyone is truly welcomed.

As I reflect on it, I neither could nor would want to put the evening together without your help. You and Steve running errands and Dad doing the shopping are very helpful to me during the busy December days. You always think of things I would have overlooked or forgotten. Dad picking up

Grandma and her sisters for liturgy and dinner means the world to them: They could not otherwise come. Your pitching in when it is time to carve the turkey, serve the meal, and clear the dishes makes the evening run smoothly. It frees me so that I too can enjoy our guests. Then, when everyone is gone, helping me to put things away and unwind with conversation shortens my day and truly makes it a memorable celebration.

David, much like our previous Christmas celebrations, my early memories of Church were the priest doing the planning, the preparation, and the implementation of almost every event. As I have had to let go of the simple things, like Christmas arrangements, it has become a tiny bit easier to relinquish the bigger things, like life decisions, to you and Steve. It is very humbling, even scary, to admit that those are no longer even my decisions to make. Today, I see our priests struggling with this same challenge of letting go. They, as I, have a hard time distinguishing between what is truly essential for them to do and what someone else can not only do as well but maybe even better. Please understand that we priests and parents only want what is best for you. If we are less than enabling servants all of the time, our goal remains not to make you more dependent but to truly help you develop the security for a total dependence on God.

David, what I have written illustrates that contemporary priesthood is very much a call to a life of paradox. I think you said it well when you said that priests are not on a separate plane but they do have a unique function, role, and contribution. If they are to be teaching, sanctifying, and nourishing the people of God, formation can begin to give them the necessary skills. No education can prepare any individual for every eventuality; it can only begin to provide the security for a person to make a commitment to lifelong learning. Scripture, retreats, and quiet reflective times can be of great help in the head understanding of a Christ-centered spirituality. However, only in the daily encounters with

women and men can the heart dimension of our spiritual being
continue to unfold and grow. Gathering for Eucharist, the
source and summit of our faith, can nourish us. Yet only in
building community can we come closer to recognizing the
fullness of Jesus "in the breaking of the bread."

Going one step further, if we are to truly call our priests
to accompaniment, we need to move beyond words and theory. Since accompanying means to go with or attend, we need
to look at some specific ways we can be mutually supportive
of our priests. To do so, I have a few practical recommendations.

1. Before ordination and periodically afterwards, I think
it would be an important priestly practice to go incognito into
a Eucharistic celebration. Come early and stay awhile after
the liturgy. Ask the question: If this is where I was called to
worship, would I want to return? Why or why not? Am I doing similar things in our parish?

One of the more welcoming communities I have encountered was on vacation in a small Montana town. Your Dad
and I were greeted as we arrived, people introduced themselves, and we were specifically invited to stay for coffee and
doughnuts afterwards. But more importantly, the community, not just the presider, called us by name; we felt blessed
in the readings, songs, and reflection; we were nourished at
the inclusive table; and we were challenged to share ourselves.
This was not just a Sunday event; it was their way of life.
Yes, it took time, but I have not forgotten the celebration,
though it was years ago, and I would want to return again
and again.

2. Every seven years, the priest needs to take a month-
long minisabbatical in a placement totally different than the
primary ministry. If the priest is pastoring, this means getting away from the everyday demands of the parish in order
to spend some time in a homeless shelter, a soup kitchen, a
residential facility for the developmentally impaired. If the
priest is teaching or in special work, it means filling in at a

parish, taking calls, attending meetings, enabling people, presiding at services.

I first learned this lesson when you were a tiny baby. As you know, I had worked in the unmarried parent program for two years after graduate school. During that time, I counseled single moms about pregnancy, childbirth and the choice of rearing the baby or relinquishing the child for adoption. It was easy to tell others what they could do, but it was altogether different when we brought you home from the hospital and I was living the reality of parenthood twenty-four hours each day. Suddenly, the best theories in the world flew out the window.

3. If the priests are to be encouraged to take minisabbaticals in different ministries, perhaps the most effective way for that to occur is in modeling. Rather than for bishops and formation personnel to always spend time in the chancery or classroom, actually spending time incognito in a parish could be very helpful. A graphic example comes to mind. In the early 1970s I was asked to help design the human-services curriculum for the community college. I had heard about a program in Chicago and went there to visit. As I sat in the classes, talked with the faculty, and brainstormed with the director, it became apparent to me that the classroom and the world had come together. I later learned that each faculty member was required to spend at least one semester every seven years doing what they were teaching the students. People who were preparing child-care staff had to actually work in a day-care setting. The theories of teaching children, conducting parent meetings, and balancing budgets moved from "This is what you should do" to "These are some very concrete things that I found effective in meeting the challenge."

4. Continuing education must be a priority for priests, and, from my experience, I would suggest that periodically a college class be taken with young students.

The theological ethics class I took with you last summer was an eye-opener for me. Though my master's degree has been supplemented by workshops and conferences these past twenty-six years, some of your questions reminded me that you, a member of the current generation, have grown up in a totally different setting. You had difficulty talking about pre–Vatican II because it was not your experience: You had not yet been born.

The class also helped me to appreciate the variety of people being called to ministry. Hearing the widowed seminarian in his fifties talk about his foster child gave new meaning to the Beatitudes. The attorney's overview of the legal dimensions in physician-assisted suicide raised a number of new considerations. All of these conversations only highlighted how, in this highly technological world when we think we have the answers, even the questions are changing.

5. David, this next suggestion comes from my heart though my head tells me it would be difficult to implement. It is that periodically the priest needs to live with a family for at least a week. In addition to getting to know them as people, it could be of great help in developing new norms for keeping prayer a life priority regardless of vocation.

Over the years, monastic prayer has been the model: time alone, quiet reflection, the desert experience. In my own life, when I would see Bishop Bernard Topel here in Spokane, he would often ask me how my prayer life was. I remember responding that with a four- and a two-year-old, all I asked was for three minutes of uninterrupted quiet just to read a recipe. Before he died in 1986, I was able to tell him that while I did not always find quiet time, I had come to a profound awareness of Christ in my life through my family, my parish, and my work in Catholic Charities. In sharing these experiences with him, we both grew in our understanding of the kinds and times of prayer.

6. One of the most important recommendations I could offer to any priest is to have a prayer group not just of clergy but rather one that models Church. This suggestion comes

from my own treasured experience. After thinking about it for some time, last year a layman, two laywomen, two priests, and a woman religious agreed to form a mixed prayer group. We share prayer, review what is going on in our lives, and celebrate the Eucharist. Modeling Church, the group has become very meaningful to each one of us.

At one of our gatherings, during the review of life, an attorney shared deep feelings about serving as a Eucharistic minister. She reflected on the variety of hands that are extended to her: shriveled, dirty, tiny, well manicured. As she spoke, the priests in the group were visibly moved. They had forgotten some of the wonder of their work.

7. Especially during the decade of the nineties I recommend that every priest make a preferential option for laypeople. As it has been with you and Steve, letting go is never easy. If we really believed that every person is called to service, think what the creative energy of 99 percent of the Catholic Church might achieve in our troubled world!

I have been in the social-service field for twenty-five years. In that arena, we have continually added new programs in an attempt to deal with a problem: apartments for the elderly and handicapped, a soup kitchen for the homeless, child abuse prevention for the potential victims of abuse and neglect. In this same period of time, I have only seen an increase in the number of people who are homeless, hungry, and abused. Like a funnel, society has been telling everyone to refer those in need to social-service agencies. In short, we have been willing to pass the problem on to someone else. In accompaniment, we must ask not what should I do but rather how can I enable others? In so doing, we can invert the funnel, spreading out the numbers of people called to respond in enabling others to make choices, to gain some control over their own lives.

8. David, my final recommendation relates to my own growing awareness of the interdependence of all people in our global world. When Mount Saint Helen erupted, the ash from

Washington State was deposited around the world. If we are to be responsive to the needs of all people, both our priests and people must have an appreciation of our multicultural, multilingual world. Study is important, but living with the people is priceless.

When I was in Tanzania with the Catholic Relief Services staff and volunteers earlier this year, we visited a women's center to talk about their self-help projects. The women were excited because they had saved the equivalent of $40 toward their goal of $7,000 for a child care center. As I heard their story, I looked down at my blue-and-white-striped sweater for which I had paid $39.95 shortly before I left Spokane. I now carry the needs of these women and their children with me. How to both change my life-style and join in solidarity with them has not fully unfolded, but I am altogether different after having walked with them.

David, this letter, like so many of my others, cannot be completed but rather can only be continued. In priesthood, as in parenting, new insights continue to evolve. In my life I have been accompanied by people who have been learning teachers, wounded healers, enabling servants. Some of them were lay, some religious, and some ordained. For your future, it is my prayer that the stereotypes and imposed expectations will be washed away from all and that your life will be even more richly blessed because you have been able to share with such people of faith.

> My love comes to you—
> Mom

About the Contributors

MATTHEW H. CLARK, D.D., was born and raised in the Diocese of Albany and served as a priest of that diocese for seventeen years. He received both the S.T.L. and the J.C.L. from the Gregorian University in Rome. From 1974 to 1979 he was spiritual director for the North American College in Rome. In 1979 he was named bishop of Rochester, New York, where he presently serves.

DONALD B. COZZENS, priest and pastoral psychologist, is vicar for clergy and religious in the Diocese of Cleveland. For over twenty years he has ministered to priests and religious as spiritual director, counselor, and retreat master. He holds an M.A. from the University of Notre Dame and a Ph.D. from Kent State University. His articles and reviews have appeared in *Cistercian Studies*, *Horizons*, *Human Development*, *The Notre Dame Magazine*, and *Emmanuel*.

DONALD J. GOERGEN, O.P., is a Dominican priest and presently serves as provincial for the Province of Saint Albert the Great. He is a systematic theologian and taught theology for ten years at the Aquinas Institute of Theology (St. Louis). In addition to many articles, his publications include *The Sexual Celibate*, *The Power of Love*, *The Mission and Ministry of Jesus*, and *The Death and Resurrection of Jesus*.

DONNA M. HANSON is presently secretary for social ministries for the Diocese of Spokane. Her life and work are the subject of an article entitled "A Voice for the U.S. Laity" in the September 1988 issue of *St. Anthony Messenger*. The magazine called Hanson "one of the most prominent Catholic lay persons in the United States." The article was written a year after Hanson addressed Pope John Paul II on behalf of the American Catholic laity in San Francisco on September 18, 1987. Hanson holds a master's in social work from St. Louis University.

PATRICIA H. LIVINGSTON, a Catholic laywoman and mother of three young adults, is the associate director of the Center for Continuing Formation in Ministry at the University of Notre Dame. A counselor and nationally known speaker, she has given workshops and lectures in the area of sexuality and relationships to priests and religious for ten years. She was given the 1990 U.S. Catholic Award for furthering the cause of women in the Church.

PAUL J. PHILIBERT, O.P., currently Dominican provincial for the Province of Saint Martin de Porres, has taught theology for many years, including being professor of moral theology at Saint Mary's Seminary (Roland Park) in Baltimore and professor of moral theology and religious development at The Catholic University of America. He was also president of the Dominican School of Philosophy and Theology in Berkeley, California. He has published many articles in the areas of religious ethics and spirituality.

DAVID N. POWER, O.M.I., is a native of Dublin, Ireland. He holds an S.T.D. from the Pontifical Liturgical Institute, San Anselmo, Rome. Since 1977 he has been professor of systematic theology and liturgy at The Catholic University of America. He has written a number of books including *Ministers of Christ and His Church*; *Christian Priest: Elder and Prophet*; *Gifts That Differ: Lay Ministries Established and Unestablished*; *Unsearchable Riches: The Symbolic Nature of Liturgy*; *The Sacrifice We Offer: The Tridentine Dogma and Its Reinterpretation*; and *Liturgy and Culture*.

REMBERT G. WEAKLAND, O.S.B., archbishop of Milwaukee since 1977, chaired the National Conference of Catholic Bishops' *ad hoc* Committee, which drafted the Bishops' Pastoral Letter: *Economic Justice for All: Pastoral Letter on Catholic Social Teaching and the U.S. Economy* (approved and accepted by the NCCB full body on November 18, 1986). He presently serves as chair of the NCCB's Committee on Ecumenical and Interreligious Affairs.

EVELYN EATON WHITEHEAD is a developmental psychologist. She holds a doctorate from the University of Chicago. Her professional work focuses on issues of adult maturity, the dynamics of leadership, and the social analysis of community and parish life. JAMES D. WHITEHEAD is a pastoral theologian and historian of religion. He received a doctorate from Harvard University. His theological interests concern questions of contemporary spirituality, ministerial leadership, and theological method in ministry. The Whiteheads are consultants in education and ministry through Whitehead Associates, which they established in 1978. Jim and Evelyn have been associated with the Institute of Pastoral Studies at Loyola University in Chicago since 1970. From 1973 to 1978 they were members of the graduate theological faculty at the University of Notre Dame. They have coauthored several books, the most recent of which is *The Promise of Partnership: Leadership and Ministry in an Adult Church*. Their earlier book *A Sense of Sexuality: Christian Love and Intimacy* received the Book-of-the-Year Award from the journal *Human Development*.